INCREATE LIGHT

OTHER BOOKS BY ERIC RHODE

Tower of Babel

A History of the Cinema from Its Origins to 1970

On Birth & Madness

The Generations of Adam

Psychotic Metaphysics

On Intuition, Hallucination and the Becoming of "O"

Plato's Silence

Notes on the Aniconic

Axis Mundi

On Revelation

Silence and the Disorder of Tongues

Himalaya

Psychotic Metaphysics, second edition

INCREATE LIGHT

Eric Rhode

APEX ONE

First published in 2021
by Apex One
7 Hillsleigh Road,
London W8 7LE

British Library Cataloguing in Publication Data

A C.I.P. for this book is available from the British Library

ISBN: 978–0–9935100–8–3

Edited by Communication Crafts
Designed by Bradbury & Williams

Much later (meaning any time after Homer), the mystery of vision produced strange theories.

[ONIANS, 1951: 73]

Logos: *semina aeternitatis*: increate light

Now, far above here the light that shines from heaven on the
backs of everything, on the backs of all things, in the very
highest of high worlds – it is clearly the same light here within
a man. We see it when, on touching a body, we feel the warmth
within it. We hear it when we press our ears shut, we hear
something like a hum and the noise of a blazing fire. One
should venerate this light as something seen and heard. Anyone
who knows this will become handsome and famous!

[CHANDOGYA UPANISHAD, 3.13.7–8]

Being itself is first and last. It is eternal and utterly present. It
is utterly perfect and ultimate. It is utterly one and is so in all
ways. If you wonder at these things with a pure mind, you will
be filled with a greater light.

[ST BONAVENTURE OF BAGNOREGIO, *ITINERARIUM MENTIS IN DEUM*
(CH. 6 IN BROWN, 1993)]

One must not try to discover where it comes from. For there
is not any 'where'. It neither comes from nor goes anywhere,
it both appears and does not appear. For this reason, it is
necessary not to pursue it, but to remain in stillness, until it
should appear, preparing oneself to be a contemplator, just as
the eye awaits the rising sun.

[PLOTINUS, *ENNEAD* 5.5.8]

God will make the teaching perfect in the day of eternity, where all is light. What I know of God, that is light: what touches creatures is night. That is the true light that has no contact with creatures. What one knows must be light. St. John says, 'God is a true light that shines in darkness.' What is this darkness? Firstly, that a man should cling to nothing and hang on to nothing, be blind and know nothing of creatures. I have said before, 'He who would see God must be blind.' Secondly, 'God is a light that shines in the darkness.' He is a light that blinds us. That means a light of such nature cannot be comprehended; it has no end and knows no end. The blinding of the soul means that she knows nothing and is aware of nothing. The third 'darkness' is best of all and means that there is no light.

[IN WALSHE, 2009: 460].

Lord in Thy light shall we know the light. (Psalm 36:9)

[QUOTED BY MEISTER ECKHART (IN WALSHE, 2009: 70)]

The soul cannot surpass herself with the light that God has given her, for it is her own, presented to her by God as a bridal gift, into the soul's highest power. Although this light is in the likeness of God, yet it is created by God, for the Creator is one and the light is another, and is creature: for before god created any creatures, God was there but no light and no darkness.

[IN WALSHE, 2009: 315]

Paul rose from the ground and with open eyes saw nothing (Acts 9:8). Our masters (Albertus Magnus) say that heaven has a light within itself, and yet it does not shine. [...] Seeing nothing, he saw God. The light that is God flows out and darkens every light. [...] In seeing nothing, he saw the divine Nothing.

[*IBID.*: 137–141]

*There is a power in the soul which alone is free. Sometimes
I have called it the guardian of the spirit, sometimes I have
called it the light of the spirit, sometimes I have said it is a little
spark. But now I say that it is neither this nor that; and yet it
is something more exalted. [...] The citadel of the soul. Take
the lowest angel in his pure nature: the smallest splinter or
spark that ever fell from him would suffice to light up the whole
world with bliss and joy.*

[*IBID.*: 63]

*The simple and absolute and unchangeable mysteries of
theology lie hidden in a prefulgent blanket of darkness as it
were, a darkness of silence that secretly teaches the sacred
truths. And where it seems darkest, this darkness radiates
light in abundance beyond measure. For what can in no way
be touched or seen fills intellects there in abundance with
splendours more than beautiful; it is as though all the intellects
have been made captive to their eyes.*

[ST PSEUDO-DIONYSIUS THE AEROPAGITE, PRAYER TO THE TRINITY
(IN ALLEN, 2015: 11)]

René Descartes: *I would like to gaze in wonder and adoration on the beauty of this immense light, so far as the eye of my darkened intellect can bear it.*

[THIRD MEDITATION (IN COTTINGHAM, STOOTHOFF, & MURDOCH, 1984: 36)]

Thomas Hobbes (*in answer*): *The phrase 'a great light in the intellect' is metaphorical, and so has no force in argument. Moreover, anyone who is free from doubt claims he has such a 'great light' and has no less strong a propensity of the will to affirm what he has no doubt about than someone who possesses real knowledge.*

René Descartes: *It is quite irrelevant whether the phrase 'a great light' has force in the argument or not; what matters is whether it helps to explain matters – and it does. As everyone knows, a 'light in the intellect' means transparent clarity of cognition; and while perhaps not everyone who thinks he possesses this does in fact possess it, this does not prevent its being quite different from a stubborn opinion which is formed in the absence of any evidential perception.*

[IBID.: 134–135]

Light as an idea, as well as an experience, signifies a point of intersection in thought, sometimes associated with beginnings, and at other times with imaginary/real extensions in space that naturally are inseparable from ideas concerning time. Knowing whether the light that I am thinking about is numinous/real or increate/created, or a light associated with the physical world/a light of the mind/a light that in some way directs my attention towards a transcendental that is inseparable from states of acute anxiety. ('Increate' can signify an association of light with an idea of the eternal, which can be tormentingly opaque in significance.) The 'great and terrible idea of eternity' thought Nicolas Malebranche (1674, quoted in Melamed, 2016: v). For the poet and philosopher Paul Valéry the concept of eternity is without meaning and so of use in indicating the presence of an unknowable in poetry: which is an interesting idea, but not one that I intend to follow. My primary interest is to think about the meaning of mind as having an innate history in the contemplative life. The intention is to explore a theme that I am largely ignorant about by means of a type of reverie–diary.

Natural light could signify a light of the mind, which by way of the 'nature' in 'natural' is related to the created world. Or it may, in spite of the reference to nature, signify a type of light that has no relation to theories concerning creation. But here the difficulties begin. All definitions are forms of measure, and I have no way of knowing how to think about the immeasurable. In terms of psychoanalysis (one of my points of departure in writing this book), I value Bion's conjecture concerning the becoming of 'O' as a definition in which 'O' is a cypher that in a somewhat inscrutable and Bionic way gives expression to the indefinable.

In Bion's description, 'becoming' has an adjectival relation to 'O' in the form of the becoming of 'O'. In order to explore the ramifications of the contemplative, I need to separate 'becoming' from 'O' and think of 'becoming' separately before I think of it inherent in the contemplative. In so far as Bion's 'O' makes itself known by means of 'becoming', so eternity, as the 'increate' in 'increate light', intimates by its presence an unusual and complex sign language in relation to light and in the possible relations of light to diaphanous or semi-transparent means of transmission (fabrics, stained-glass windows, clouds).[1] 'Glory' is a term that signifies 'increate light', as in Wordsworth's phrase 'clouds of glory'. I associate such clouds with the cloud of unknowing of fourteenth-century English mysticism, as representing a condition of breakdown as well as of breakthrough. I posit three cosmologies: a cosmology related to the increate, a cosmology related to the created, and as an interim the cloud cosmology or womb place of Exodus, into which Moses was able to enter and to meditate. Plato is not alone among philosophers in thinking of a similar dimension as being a spiritual means of transmigration between lives: a belief that I do not subscribe to, although I believe in associating the innate with a type of

---

[1] The dependence of light on something other than itself if it is to be realised in creation is not universally true, and yet the fact is of great importance that there should be multiple examples of such a dependence (as I intend to show). It is essential to the inspiration of the Annunciation narrative, which as the key paradigm to this book is a fundamental interpretation of the coming together of the good objects in Kleinian theory. The physicist Arthur Zajonc has described how natural light will appear as a total darkness if there is nothing, not even a mote of dust, on which it can depend as a means to realise itself as light. St ps.-Dionysius, among other theologians, has recognised as aspects of an otherwise secluded deity the affinity that exists between a light that is increate and a darkness that is vibrant (Zajonc, 1955).

culture that is informative of future knowledge, while being itself unformed. The cloud is a residual memory of something that the conscious mind may be unaware of.[2]

Freud centred his interest on the life of adults and on drawing a radius of light around the richness or poverty of these lives. Melanie Klein centred her interest on the life of a child, and with a similar radius, had the child at its centre. Esther Bick centred her interest on the possible intimacies of mother and newborn, an intimacy that can take on cosmological proportions in thought of a microscopic kind. I believe that Wilfred Bion and Donald Meltzer centred their interest on an even earlier stage in the history of our life: on the fluency of meaning that exists in relation to changes in thought at the time of being innate and then born, spiritually as well as actually. If I look into the mirror of life, I may catch a glimpse of an idea of eternity that disappears if I try to define it. Clouds of unknowing and clouds of glory are

---

[2] For a compelling and different view of the cloud as a means for metaphysical reflection, see the following: 'Our initial withdrawal from wrong and erroneous ideas of God is a transition from darkness to light. Next comes an awareness of hidden things that guides the soul through sense phenomena to the world of the invisible. And this awareness is a kind of cloud, which overshadows all appearances, and slowly guides and accustoms the soul to look towards what is hidden. Next the soul makes progress through all these stages and goes on higher, and as she leaves below all that human nature can attain, she enters within the secret chamber of the divine knowledge, and here she is cut off on all sides by the divine darkness. Now she leaves behind her all that can be grasped by sense or reason, and the only thing left for her contemplation is the invisible and the incomprehensible (Gregory of Nyssa, Sermon 11, in Daniélou 1962: 247).

A mystic during the Middle Ages quipped that 'sacred ecstasies can induce a pleasant cloud of unknowing, and from amazement at such a stupendous new experience, they can cause a mist of grateful forgetting' (in Newman 2005: 12).

companions in a relationship with an eternal something that knowledge has no access to.

Increate light as a presence marks an entry of the unpermitted into the permitted. It can reveal itself by way of pronouncements that are conflicted in meaning, as when St ps.-Dionysius refers to God oxymoronically as a 'ray of darkness' – a light so brilliant that it can be seen only by way of an unusual (i.e. vibrant) darkness. Sometimes incoherence presents itself as a form of speech. Wilfred Bion's intuition concerning a tennis-net that visually alternates between being a luminous reticulation against dark background or a dark reticulation against a luminous background has its source in a similar trains of thought.[3] The alternation of light and dark in relation to the tennis-net is a version of the 'ray of darkness' idea. And so, Plato:

> *Stranger:* The Sophist takes refuge in the darkness of not-Being where he is at home and has the knack of feeling his way, and it is in the darkness of the place that makes him so hard to perceive.
>
> *Theaetetus:* That may well be.
>
> *Stranger:* Whereas the philosopher, whose thoughts constantly dwell upon the nature of reality, is difficult to see because his region is so bright. For the eye of most of us cannot endure keeping our gaze fixed on the divine.
>
> [*THE SOPHIST* 254 A & B]

---

[3] I conjecture that contemplation as the ground for any exchange within a transference intimates some kind of theology. Is 'transference', which most people find mysterious, a way of describing God?

With Plotinus rather than Plato in mind, I would have 'O' be a symbol that eludes any attempt to define it (which, I suppose, is a definition of sorts) while, at the same time, as being a presence generative of meaning. It is a fountain that is perceptible through its overflow into the basin of the intelligible or *Nous* (which is a stage in the formation of a meaning that is inseparable from the radiance of 'O'). The brilliance of increate light is overpowering and is a characteristic that sets it apart it from the meaning of natural light.

Being as true life is inaccessible to knowledge; that which is perceived is not knowledge. What Moses yearned for is satisfied by the very things that leave his desire unsatisfied.

[GREGORY OF NYSSA, THE LIFE OF MOSES: 236 (QUOTED BY NES, 2007: 142)]

With good reason, the age we live in idealises the idea of knowledge and the capacity of thought to assess the values of the knowable. This is a matter for gratitude. And yet attention, when directed in this way, can distract mind from recognising the potent existence of the unknowable – that which to some extent exists in opposition to acts of knowing. The idea of God is an example of such an opposition. God is not an episteme; God cannot be known. Similarly, according to Gregory of Nyssa, 'Being' cannot be known. Belief or disbelief in the supernatural has at most a tenuous relation to the tallies of knowledge, and statements concerning belief or disbelief in the existence of transcendental forms are of little value. Theories concerning the relation of increate light to creation sometimes describe oppositions and sometimes reconciliations: but who can be sure? Against the positivism of the age, I am drawn to those who tell me that there is a supernatural light so brilliant that it can appear as a vibrant darkness. Against the assumption that believing is a questionable activity, I still incline to believe in the existence of a reality that has no relation to powers of understanding.

A relation between natural light and a light of the mind, as when the light of the mind is conceived as inspiration, can give the (erroneous?) impression of being increate light.

Albert Einstein himself tells us that probably in 1896, as a sixteen-year old, he had the impossible thought that if one runs after a light wave with the velocity equal to that of light, then the light wave would stop. [...]

The paradox of running with light would simply not leave his imagination. [...] For nearly ten years he harboured the puzzle. During that time, he matured scientifically. [...] His question concerning the nature of light was the irritating nucleus around which grew the pearl of relativity. [...] A new thought form was shaped: it has become known as Einstein's special theory of relativity.

[ZAJONC, 1955: 253–254]

Again and ever again, it is ourselves whom we study in studying light.

[IBID.: 329]

Certain seeds of truth are naturally in our soul. [...] God has given us a light to distinguish truth from falsehood. [...] (He) did not place a rational soul in the body. (Rather) he kindled a fire without light in the heart.

[DESCARTES, *DISCOURSE ON METHOD* (IN COTTINGHAM, STOOTHOFF, & MURDOCH, 1985)]

We are born to be a burning and shining light, and whatever men learn of others, they see in the light of others' souls.

[THOMAS TRAHERNE, 'THE THIRD CENTURY' (IN *CENTURIES OF MEDITATIONS)*]

A physicist, a doctor, a theologian and an artist will think differently about the meaning of light, whether the light is of a created or increate sort. Apart from their different views, each of which may be useful as well as sensible, there is an issue concerning the numinous, which all of them may wish to set aside, on the grounds that it appears to derive from the multiple contradictions that relate to an idea of an increate insecurely defined as being the eternal.

1. *An understanding in terms of nature:* I need to discover a source for radiance as a presence in nature if I am going to be able to measure the radiance, even though its realisation appears to exist in an idea of time and space that cannot be measured.

2. *An understanding in terms of psychology:* Increate light is a light of the mind that is brought to conscious attention by events in the mind that may be conscious or unconscious or it may be brought to conscious attention by way of a visionary experience (as in a Platonic perception of beauty).

3. *An understanding in terms of theology:* Some people by way of acts of contemplation think to perceive the godhead in the form of visions of increate light. I have no reason to doubt them, although I have not had any such experience myself. Thinking that 'it can be true only if I have experienced it' strikes me as an inadequate response in this circumstance.

Increate light in terms of the Genesis creation myth has to be other than the natural light that the deity creates on the third day, since the creation of natural light necessarily occurs within a prior establishment of a space–time model. I must ask myself whether I am thinking in terms of a metaphysical idea, or whether I am thinking about techniques that enable me to explore the meaning of experience as it occurs within the mythologies of nature. To think of Plato's allegory of the Cave and the Sun, with looking into the sun as defining the numinous is to misunderstand the problem. The metaphor that brings together the idea of increate light with the light of the sun is misleading. But Plato does provide a wonderful image for the increate light when he has his hero, Er, who has entered the company of the dead (even though he is still alive), travel through a cosmic pillar of light, seemingly immeasurable in its perpendicular ascent[1] in the journey of transmigration that the dead have to make as they leave one life as a stage in progress towards another.[2] In either case, visions of light are inseparable from ideas of being directed and of travelling. Is the making of journeys of an imaginative or of a supernatural kind marginal to an experience of actual seeing?

At a late stage in working on this text, I come to see that revelation as a companion to the contemplative has put itself forward covertly as means of explanation. Contemplation signifies hints and allusions that may or may not form into a steady and inward-seeming unfolding of meaning. But revelation is the companion to states of discontinuity. Mind may have to travel 'through strange seas of thought alone', as William Wordsworth realised in describing the mind/statue of Newton in a later version of *The Prelude* ('By your light we see the light', *Psalm 36*). Revelation does not acknowledge the existence of intermediaries; it eclipses subject and object. The physicist Robert Oppenheimer, overawed by evidence of the power of nuclear fission, recalled a quotation from the *Bhagavad Gita* (in a version of the text that I do not have): 'I am become Death, the destroyer of worlds.'

---

[1] The idea of a pillar of increate light that may originate from within the earth and rise up to some inconceivable heavenly height occurs in many mythologies.

[2] The vast pillar of light image has its likeness in at least two Indian myths: both Krishna/Vishnu and Shiva appear in different contexts as immense pillars of light.

In contemplation there is usually an intermediary, a subject, initially mind itself. Any light that I might perceive will present itself as a light of the mind. Intermediaries have no place in this context. There is only an indefinable radiance. Knowledge is slow in gathering itself together in the contemplative mind; and revelation inhibits this process, especially when it has the inscrutable form of 'O'.[3]

Someone might say: you are thinking about the idea of 'a light of the mind'. Are you thinking about a light in your mind or, assuming there is a god, are you thinking about a light in God's mind? I answer by saying I have no way of knowing. If there is no God, where do I find the light in myself?

> The essential true nature of all existing things is light. It is not logically possible that the essential nature of all existing things not be the light [of existence]. And that light is unitary because it is impossible for it to become other than what it essentially is. Thus, neither space nor time can sunder its essential unity because indeed their essential unity is nothing but that light. And so the light is one, and that light is consciousness.
>
> [THE SHIVAITE SEER AND PHILOSOPHER ABHINAVAGUPTA (QUOTED IN MULLER-ORTEGA, 2004: 54)]

---

[3] St Gregory Palamas proposes that grace or the Holy Spirit, to which he gives a masculine definition, initiates the ability to perceive increate light. The indication of grace heightens focus on the existence of that which is incomprehensible: a focus on the wind that bloweth where it listeth. '[...] The very comprehension a man may have, he possesses incomprehensibly. [...] the spirit by whom he sees is incomprehensible' (*The Triads*, in Meyendorff, 1983: 34).
Do you not understand that in place of the intellect, the eyes and ears, they acquire the incomprehensible Spirit and by Him hear, see and comprehend? [*ibid.*: 35]

The divine cannot be taught in words like the other things we have learnt. But from daily application to the subject itself and from communion with it, suddenly, as by a fiery spark, light, in having been ignited in the rational soul, now nourishes itself.

[PLATO, *LETTERS*, 7.341[1]]

The activity of intellect, which is contemplative, seems to be superior in worth (to the practical life) and to aim at no end beyond itself. [...] It is not in so far as he is man that he will live so, but in so far as something divine is present in him.

[ARISTOTLE, *NICOMACHEAN ETHICS*, BOOK 10: 1177B15-28]

Clark Heinrich (1995: 191–198) reports eating the fly agaric mushroom every day for a month in 1977. After initial experiences of nausea and discomfort, he (and his friend) finally obtained a magnificent, revelatory experience. Heinrich was absorbed into the unsurpassable light of the Godhead. Attempting to repeat the experience, he eagerly ate the mushrooms a few days later, only to be plunged into hell (quoted in Clark, 2019: 109).

Krishna: the scent and taste of the sacred plant Soma, which I become, is the wandering moon.

[BHAGAVAD GITA, 15: 13]

---

[1] It is questionable whether or not Plato wrote this letter.

Soma is a god/goddess, as well as a possibly edible substance. Granting the victim of the sacrifice the status of being divine, if only for a day, depends on the extent to which the victim is edible. The ideology of the sacrifice grants status to acts of cannibalism.

Aristotle observes a divine element in the contemplative life (*theoria*) and so esteems it more highly than he does *praxis*, or the commitment to a life of projects or to the facts of *doing*.[2] An indefinable 'something', within a contemplative formation, enables movement from one definition into another.[3] It puts the contemplative at risk by taking it from a phenomenological or knowable condition into conditions in which there may be no knowing, only states of disorientation. Is the divine element in the contemplative to be valued as encouraging thought or as a form of distraction, or even as an incitement to states of delusion?

A great Plotinus scholar, Father Jean Trouillard, claimed that: 'Contemplation is not speculation. There is in contemplation as *theoria* something more intuitive and more transforming than there is in the learned speculations of present-day thinking. *To contemplate is to become*' (Trouillard,

---

[2] This is comparable to a Bible *visio dei*. 'Lord, lift up the light of thy countenance upon us' (Psalm, 4.6). Aristotle responds to the possible entry of a *visio dei* into contemplation as though this were a matter of fact or as an apprehension that invites a bland response. In fact, the more I think about it, the entry of this apparent stranger into ordinary thought processes is potentially terrifying. I think in the same way of the entry into my thought processes of Bion's 'O'.

[3] If the divine element in contemplation is evocative of a foetus in the womb of thought, it is as a foetus in no ordinary pregnancy. It is like the increate light that the archangel Gabriel installed in the womb of the virgin mother.

1972; my italics). Plotinus sometimes, or perhaps always, considers the cosmos to be a system of thought only marginally related to matter (which is believed to be evil). Is there a particular type of contemplation that activates becoming; and if this is the case, how would I know it? The act of contemplation, however much it might be depended on, has a feeling about it of the strange, even of the alien. It can convey an impression of floating in an unbounded state. To enter it can be to be without a sense of having entered anything. Meaning as a container seems to be in a continuous state of being emptied and re-filled. Hesychast monks, and Zen monks similarly, think of contemplation as inseparable from a need to train bodily posture, often over-strenuously. Other people may open themselves to the contemplative and in doing so may experience a stirring of music within a sense of absence; and yet there may be no sound. Elusive, indefinable, the contemplative has a touch of the regressed about it, even of the awkward and illicit.

In a room in which there is a single person, there is always the possible presence of thought. If someone else enters the room, there is a division of psychic space. In making a case for dismissing religious perspectives as illusory, Freud opened unexpected vistas in religious thought that otherwise were unexplored. 'Increate' – as in the mysterious contradiction of the unknowable (eternity) and the potentially knowable (light) – indicates a type (or types) of immeasurable whose complex relation to measure may or may not be one of opposition. By way of 'O' and 'becoming', Aristotle's divine element enters into the field of psychoanalysis; and, once invoked, it cannot be dismissed.[4] The culture of psychoanalysis asserts that certain truths must be respected, such as 'peace at any price', even though some truths may present themselves as veiled.[5] Bion having made his cryptic announcement concerning 'O' and becoming did not explore its significance; he moved on into other fields for thought.

It is possible to define the practical life in terms of schedules and aims in a way that does not interest the contemplative mind. Romain Rolland, in an exchange of letters with Freud, described the contemplative as oceanic. Wilfred Bion and Donald Meltzer separately recognise a shift in focus towards a visionary world of a similar kind, pre-natal, specifically the 'elsewhere' of the innate, in which 'becoming' is identified with a radiance that increasingly is set apart through the act of being born.

> The moments which seem most arid when we are living through them can be seen later as permeated with light. Following Gregory of Nyssa, I think that in the spiritual life the same experiences can be seen at first as obscure and then as luminous.
>
> [LOUIS BROUYER, INTRODUCTION TO THE SPIRITUAL LIFE, 1960: 356]

---

[4] Are these servants that won't leave the house, even though they have been dismissed...? This surely is a phantasy about one's own parents as the good objects presenting themselves in their goodness, or, alternatively, as the good objects presenting themselves in the form of surrogate parents.

[5] I see here a connection between being veiled and being blinded. I believe that I am touching on the theme of intermediaries whose value increase light endorses and that in other respects might be found damaging or inadequate.

Contemplation is like pulling up fishing nets without expectation of anything having been caught. In other terms, anchorage may be absent. And yet the hints and allusions of the contemplative can be tokens of revelation and even of a spiritual recovery.

The city of Revelations has 'no need of the sun or the moon'
(Revelation 21:23).

[GREGORY PALAMAS, *PHILOKALIA*, 4: 272]

And he showed me a pure river of water of life, clear as crystal,
proceeding out of the throne of God and of the Lamb.

[REVELATION 22¹]

[It] transformed the things it shone upon, which visible light
cannot do.

[PALAMAS, *PHILOKALIA*, 4: 276]

I have a book by Vladimir Lossky in front of me. The title of the book is *Sept jours sur les routes de France: Juin 1940* (Lossky, 1998). The reference to June 1940 drew me to the book, and I acquired a copy. In that ill-fated month, I was in France as a six-year old with my mother, father and younger brother. With difficulty, and only just, my parents enabled us to escape from France and to reach England. One memory recalls the misery of defeat: a mother in tears pushing a wheelchair with a child in it.² Vladimir Lossky writes about

---

¹ The river re-appears in Dante's *Paradiso,* Canto XXX. Cf. William Blake's picture, *Dante in the Empyrean Drinking at the River of Light,* c.1824–27.

² 'Then came the horrible month of June 1940. It was like the blow of a hammer on the head of France. The state into which the country fell can best be described as shock. Since then it got worse rather than better. In June 1940, millions upon millions of French people found themselves upon the roads, rooted away from

leaving the streets of Paris at the last moment, almost when it was too late: closed shutters, heat, dust and empty streets, a sense that the enemy was close to taking over the city. Either by hitch-hiking or by foot, and under the continuous threat of death, he made his way to southwest France to re-meet his family. During the journey he took notes in which, among other subjects, he wrote about the beauty of France, especially the beauty of its cathedrals and churches. I found his account moving, and, compelled by a depth in feeling and by a certain quality of personality in the writing, I read all Lossky's other published texts. I think his experience of his revelation of beauty while under great threat is one of the factors that underlies the formation of this book. Lossky died in 1958, at the age of 55.

His commitment to the Russian Orthodox Church conveys an unbounded sense of inspiration. He gave me a sense of mind as having directions that I knew little about. It was in his writings that I came across a commitment to the idea of increate light as a central aspect to existence and hence as the starting point for this book. Increate light for Lossky was 'a datum for mystical experience' (1959: 58). It 'is not a sensible or intelligible light; it is the light of grace'. 'Gnosis, the highest stage of awareness of the divine, is an experience of increate light. The experience itself is light: "in thy light, we shall see light"' (Lossky, *Mystical Theology*, 1944: 218).

their homes, bewildered, roofless, hungry quite unable to understand what was being done to them. [...] France was not prepared for such a misery' (Weil, 2019, Vol. 1: 76).

'Grace as light and as the source of revelation cannot remain within us unperceived' (*ibid.*, 225). Of this I am not so sure.

Lossky is inspired by a tradition that is uncompromising in its judgment on those who misunderstand the meaning of increate light. St Gregory Palamas, who lived in the fourteenth century, is the principal advocate in any question concerning this issue.

> Anyone who maintains that the light that shone about the disciples on Mount Tabor was an apparition or a symbol of the kind that now is and now is not, but has no real being and is an effect that not only does not surpass comprehension, but is inferior to it, is someone who contends against the doctrine of the saints. In their hymns and their writings, the saints call this light ineffable, uncreated, eternal, timeless, unapproachable, boundless, infinite, limitless, invisible to angels and to men, archetypal and unchanging beauty, the glory of God, the glory of Christ, the glory of the Spirit, the ray of Divinity and so forth. [...] Christ was transfigured, neither by the addition of something he was not, nor by a transformation into something he was not, but by the manifestation to His disciples of what He really was. He opened their eyes, so that instead of being blinded they could see. [...] 'He shone forth like the sun' (John, 1: 9). The image is imperfect, since what is uncreated cannot be imagined in creation without diminution.

> [GREGORY PALAMAS, *THE DECLARATION OF THE HOLY MOUNTAIN. PHILOKALIA*, 4: 422][3]

---

[3] Quoting from the *Hagioritic Tome*, Lossky writes: 'The light of intelligence is different from that which is perceived by the senses; in effect, the sensible light reveals to us objects proper to our senses, whereas the intellectual light serves to

The issue of increate light has been a long-standing source of disagreement.[4] Increate light, in so far as I can understand it, involves a *reaching out* into a nowhere that is sensed to be everywhere, or it is a *reaching inwardly and indefinitely* into the self. It is as though the self were infinite: which in a sense it is, if I see it as I do, as including a sentient pre-natal life in the womb, beyond any evidence of space and time, as means of configuration that await to be released. For St Gregory Palamas and his followers increate light appears to be 'out there', as something to be arrived at or reached out to, often with the greatest difficulty. A belief that the numinous might be without location would seem to be opposed to any idea of reaching out.

In the *Phaedrus*, Plato has Socrates respond to increate light as a vision to be recalled in conditions that are other than those of a world of the born, and as a poetic reverie rather than a religious invocation, a return to a lost time that

---

manifest the truth which is in our thoughts. [...] Those who are worthy of it receive by grace and spiritual and supernatural strength. They perceive by their senses as well as by their intelligence that which is above all sense and all intellect. [...] How? That is not known except to God and to those who have had experience of His grace' (Lossky, 1959: 58–59).

[4] 'Certain Byzantine humanists who identified the intelligible with the divine could not make sense of a Hesychast type of contemplation, with its emphasis on a type of embodiment. Their appreciation of the beauty and order of the cosmos was informed by the fact that they were Hellenists and followers of Plato. At least one of them rationalised the cosmic symbolism by which God made Himself known in the name of Aristotle by thinking that knowledge by way of the senses was the one true knowledge. Science entails the contemplation of actual beings. They saw nothing new in Christianity. Simply, God had raised new symbols of his presence as signs without participation; for instance, the light of the transfiguration was no more than a meteorological phenomenon' (Clément, 1964: 49–50). John Meyen- dorff's *St Gregory Palamas and Orthodox Spirituality* (1974) is a useful introduction to this subject.

is other than the world of those who have been born. There is among the Platonists a belief in transmigration – between a life as lived now and a life as lived then. However, my sense of an overspill from the innate into a life of the born is not a theory that involves the idea of a transmigration; it is, rather, an extension of Wilfred Bion's conjecture that birth is not a caesura and that there is a flow of meaning from a 'before' into an 'after' with only death as a full stop.[5] Socrates says of the enquiring soul:

> As he beholds the beauty of this world, he recalls true beauty. [...] Every human soul by reason of its nature has had contemplation of true being; otherwise [the holy objects of vision] would never have entered it. [...] In those days [*before our present birth* – my insert] the gift of beauty in all its brightness was ours to see [in other words, this is a claim being made about the meaningful nature of innate life as belonging to theories concerning the developmental in relation to mind.] [...] We were initiated into a mystery that is accounted blessed beyond all others; whole and unblemished were we that did celebrate it, untouched by the evils that awaited us in days to come; steadfast and blissful were the spectacles on which we gazed at the moment of revelation; pure was the light that shone around us, and pure were we, without taint of that prison house that encompasses us now. Now we are as bound to our bodies as an oyster is to its shell.
>
> [*PHAEDRUS* 250B–D]

---

[5] I find myself relating the pillar of light that Er passes through as a validation of this alternative life to the rays of light emitted possibly by the eye of God in Dante's *Paradiso*.

William Wordsworth's perception of increate light as a pre-natal vision that spills over into life is word by word identical to Socrates' perception. The essential key to understanding life as it is now, as we exist in the world of the born, is a key that disappeared at the time of birth and has to be encouraged to re-appear. Our earliest years are claustrophobic because something has been lost, a suppression of visionary radiance. To be born is to begin a prison sentence that is life-long. 'Shades of the prison-house begin to close/Upon the growing Boy'. Wordsworth appears to quote Socrates. Visions of the beautiful are confused with memory; and yet the memories, grief-struck, enable those who have been born to realise their loss.

> Whither is fled the visionary gleam?
> Where is it now, the glory and the dream?
> Our birth is but a sleep and a forgetting:
> The Soul that rises with us, our life's Star,
> Hath had elsewhere its setting,
> And cometh from afar:
> Not in entire forgetfulness,
> And not in utter nakedness,
> But trailing clouds of glory do we come
> […]
> the growing boy […] beholds the light,
>   and whence it flows,
> He sees it in his joy. […]
>
> [WILLIAM WORDSWORTH, 'ODE: INTIMATIONS OF IMMORTALITY FROM RECOLLECTIONS OF EARLY CHILDHOOD']

Wordsworth relates the clouds of glory to the 'grace' of creation ('glory', I repeat, is a term for increate light, and in this context has 'our life's Star' as a way of describing incre-ate light). He indicates modes of contemplation that the psychoanalytic imagination is now beginning to focus on; their exceptional qualities are startling. For Donald Meltzer (who, like Wilfred Bion, has cast doubt on their being a 'caesura' between life before and after birth), the new-born 'emits' clouds of glory rather than 'trails' them; in other words, the clouds that represent increate light go before, rather than after, the emerging newborn. It is as though in the act of being born, I was allowed the privilege of passing through a cloud vision similar to the cloud environment that deepened Moses' capacity to meditate.

The observer in an infant observation that I once heard about met a depressed mother-to-be in a room in which a small coal fire appeared to make no impression on a sense of desolation within an intuition of intense coldness. A fort-night later, with the baby born and present, the observer was delighted to discover that a warmth filled the room which appeared to come from the mother's joyous relationship to the newborn. The depression had disappeared into the radi-ance that the newly-born infant had brought with it. In a reversal of Wordsworthian insight, the newborn had given its mother a key to escape, at least for a while, from a spiritual prison. It was as though the newborn had been able to bring a precious inheritance with it into the world of the born.

In terms of a creationist view of the cosmos, I may fail to see how startling the idea might be of a creationism devoid of increase light. For John Milton, increate light is the light of inspiration and accompanies natural light to a different purpose in the act of divine creation. In his blindness, which signifies an absence of any access to natural light, John Milton hopes that the light of inspiration will enable him to invoke the first creation – invoking the power of supernatural eyes by means of the rising world of waters dark and deep, as though the translucent waters were the waters of the eye itself, an optic for looking inwards as well as outwards.

> Hail holy light, offspring of heaven first born,
> Or of the eternal co-eternal beam
> May I express thee unblamed? Since God is light,
> And never but in unapproachèd light
> Dwelt from eternity, dwelt then in thee,
> Bright effluence of bright essence increate.
> Or hearst thou rather pure ethereal stream,
> Whose fountain who shall tell? Before the sun,
> Before the heavens thou wert, and at the voice
> Of God, as with mantle did invest
> The rising world of waters dark and deep;
> Won from the void and formless infinite.
>
> […] but thou
> Revisitst not these eyes, that roll in vain
> To find thy piercing ray, and find no dawn. […]
>
> [*PARADISE LOST*, BOOK 3, LINES 1–24]

What is emerging out of the present, in this case an entire cosmos, seemingly emerges out of an otherwise inaccessible past. What pours forward as a creation in time and space, all verb and no noun, is able to do so because like a spiritual telescope, it reveals the past as a journey backwards in time while thinking to invoke or create the future. There is no cut-off point to mark the present moment. I take this to be an implicit issue in seventeenth-century thought, as in John Locke's belief that a void in place of thought and feeling characterises prenatal life and the act of being born.

An empiricism that idealises the idea of experience by assuming that experience is acquired at the expense of something other than itself, is like an imaginary tree that is believed to flourish in spite of being uprooted.[6] John Locke, as a qualified and respected doctor as well as a philosopher, presumably wished to bring scientific scruple to bear on the practice of observation: but on at least one occasion his ability to observe was inhibited. He came to the view – he does not say how – that the infant at birth, or shortly after being born, gave little or no evidence of having a mind. He thought that any evidence of mind at birth was comparable, more or less, to a *tabula rasa*, or working surface wiped clean, on which a nurturer or instructor might impress an education.[7] No evidence that I know of supports the assumption of a vacuity or mental absence at the time of birth. It could be that Locke was responding casually to the belief (from which the unfortunate transmigration theory is drawn) that souls between lives transmigrate from one body to another.

---

[6] The flames of the burning bush that Moses encounters burn without need for fuel. In this, they reveal themselves to be an example of increate light. Locke's understanding of experience seems to me to be a substitution for the significance of increate light as being without a source.

[7] No evidence of light within this face; and yet potentially all faces give evidence of a light.

According to the Plato of *Republic* Book X, a soul, if virtuous, may be granted a vision of increate light as a token of liberation from the disagreeable imperative to travel into a new life. But the belief that the souls of the dead travel into the bodies that await their arrival is different from the belief that the individual is born with a mind vibrant with a sense of the future. Socrates in the *Meno* attempts to demonstrate that knowledge of a geometric kind can be extracted from the mind of someone who has no training in geometry; the knowledge is innate, and birth in no way interferes with it. Seeing himself as the spiritual equivalent of a midwife, Socrates thought to give birth to ideas that he believed were latent in the minds of those whom he hoped to inspire.[8]

I assume that Wilfred Bion was not trying to deny the existence of spiritual or physical crises before, or during, or after birth: rather, that he was observing continuities in cultures of reverie and dream. Biological crises may interfere with such continuities without ending them. The culture of prenatal life, although subterranean, continues to flow, while never quite disappearing.

Locke responds to a radiant vision obscurely. It was left to the visionaries and poets of the Romantic period to idealise

---

[8] In Book X of the *Republic*, Er, the noble warrior mistakenly thought to be dead, travels through states of transmigration, of a life between lives, and at one point finds himself as travelling through a vast cathedral-like pillar of light. This is a site of initiation and renewal. Passing between lives enables the Platonist to engage with truths that otherwise cannot be arrived at. The recognition of a truth that does not belong to the experience of having been born signifies a sense of revelation as related to the state of being innate.

the improbable and to look at ideas of experience uncir-
cumscribed by acts of birth and death. There is a movement
back and forth between an un-Lockeian immeasurable that
Locke reasonably distrusts and the wonderful appearance
of the Romantic sublime. Locke's implicit model is *nothing:
birth: something*. The *something* is the tutelage that the world
provides the newborn with.

Unseeing (not blindness), unhearing (not deafness) and
unknowing (not ignorance) can be outcomes of a belief in
an indefinable that realises itself in daily life, even though
it is without notation. Living out a life by way of a vision of
the unseeing is a way of indicating a necessary transience,
without which the meaning of 'living out of a life' would be
disarmed. I am unborn in the fact of having been born since a
foetal self continues to live within me. An imperceptible force
draws me to it, or impels me, in one way or another. In thinking of this kind, I am aware of being receptor to 'something',
although I do not know what this 'something' might be.
'Becoming' describes the difference between the act of being
born, or of giving birth, and a more fundamental meaning to
'being born' as a process (rather than an act) that continues
for as long as there is life. No one is completely born; being
born is an on-going process, a moment-by-moment awakening; and any presumption that birth is a singular event makes
little sense. At every stage in being, the clouds of glory are
angelic partners to the travellers through life.

The primal one created a mantra that announced: 'Let the free spaces be filled with endless light.'

[GATHA 31:7[1]]

Increate light is inseparable from the formation of a certain religious thought. I might say: in the beginning there is nature and so there is the possibility that cosmic forms might exist. Or I might say: there is increate light and so the improbable, as the sacrifice, comes into existence and in time takes on the form of being a religion or the prototype of a religion. I have to go back before any record in time, and to the upper-Oxus region of Turkmenistan, to sense the existence of inspirations whose source is inaccessible. Out of an unlimited and indefinable radiance, the contours of a remarkable prophet known as Zarathustra/Zoroaster form into a historical presence. The radiance has no relation to configurations in space and time. As in the case of the Prologue to the St John Gospel, logos or presence is inseparable from an idea of increate light.

While still youthful, the prophet meets with certain gods.

---

[1] A Zoroastrian text.

They appear in an aura of increate light (named on this occasion as 'endless light').[2]

> At dawn he went to the river to fetch water for a hoama ceremony.[3] He waded into the river in order to draw up water, and on his return he saw on one of the banks of the river a radiant Being, who led him into the presence of Ahura Mazda and five other luminous figures. The light was so great that for a moment, and in the throes of revelation, he was unable to see his own shadow.
>
> [TRANSCRIPTION FROM BOYCE, 1979: 19]

Zarathustra has a vision within which there are supernatural beings associated with a light that has no definition, meaning it is not a light to be associated to creationism and the definitions that time and space impose on radiance. (It is not disclosed at this moment that Zarathustra, too, was born out of increate light and has lived within a perception of the angels.) He is not alone in having visions of increate light. Manes, the beloved originator of the Manichean religion who thought of himself as Jesus reborn and was a gifted painter, had a way of contemplating 'parcels of light' in the water of pools and rivers (see Ries, 1991).

Increate light can be disengaged from creation, or it can be engaged with creation through something other than itself, as, say, by means of a garment or a vitreous or diapha-

---

[2] Experiencing such a universality of light may be intolerable. See Plato's dialogue *The Sophist*.

[3] The hoama or soma plant was crushed in river water to make what may have been a psychedelic drink used in ritual.

nous substance. The narrative of the Annunciation is a useful starting point for thinking about increate light's entry into a world of substances. Increate light must engage with objects that are unviolated if there is to be a transformation. I have before me a representation of Fra Lippo Lippi's painting of the Annunciation. The angel Gabriel and a young virgin, face to face, are young people, scarcely out of childhood, caught up in a transmission of a passion. As an idea, at least, the angel is the carrier of increate light into the young woman's womb (Luke 1.26–38). (Being a messenger of increate light has the same value on one level of narrative as being a messenger of logos or seed.) Increate light engenders the man who is god out of an absence that is more present than any presence. [4] The idea of insemination has many levels of meaning, apart from its fundamental physical meaning; and the meaning that Fra Lippo Lippi discovers in it by means of a painterly configuration is basic to insight in any attempt to explore other narratives concerning the influence of increate light.

In a proto-gnostic conception of reality, the conflict between the gods of light and the gods of darkness has no end. The world into which Zoroaster has been born is a world that appears out of chaos.

> For a time out of counting, the god Ohrmazd existed in the light that some called Endless Light (namely, increate light) […] while Ahriman, the god who opposed him,

---

[4] Cf. *Kaushitaki Upanishad* 2. 'The semen, O seasons, is gathered from the radiant one.'

dwelt in Endless Darkness. Between the two gods lay
the void as a boundary. That which is on high, which
is Endless Light [...] and that which is abased, which is
Endless Darkness – were limitless. There was no means
of connecting them.

[DÊNKARD 7, CH. 2 (IN BOYCE, 1964: 45–46)]

The Annunciation narrative has many forms, and it is fundamental to the idea of a coming together of the Kleinian good objects. Impregnation by the logos as a ray of increate light is a familiar belief: an ancestor of Genghis Khan was reputedly impregnated by such a means. A beam of increate light enters into the womb of Zarathustra's grandmother and at a later time into his mother's womb.

Endless Light sped down to the sun; from the sun it sped
down to the moon; from the moon it sped down to the
stars; and from the stars it sped down to the fire in the
house of Frahim-ruvanan-Zoish. From that fire it entered
Zoish's wife, at the time when she bore the daughter who
became Zardusht's mother. People said: In the house of
Frahim-ruvanan-Zoish is a fire burning that needs no
fuel. [...] The light shines from the person of the girl.

[BOYCE, 1964: 72]

After the death and resurrection of Jesus, the meaning of increate-light insemination recurs on a more general scale. The mother of Christ accompanies the disciples to an upstairs place in a building where they can observe the descent of tongues of fire from the night sky. In effect, the presence of the mother is the determining fact in the occurrence of this mystery. The tongues of fire in their earthly descent create the potential for sites where the devout might meet, constructions spiritually of architectural authority, such as Vladimir Lossky was able to take note of as he travelled through a deteriorating landscape. (The remarkable rose window of Chartres cathedral had been put into storage for the duration of the war.)

Increate light can perform the role of orientation; it can enable the sacred to realise itself in terms of direction. It is able to authorise sites for worship and congregation. Its prototype is the womb-like chalice of the Last Supper, which is radiant with increate light. The mystery of transubstantiation in relation to this chalice is analogous to the transformation of the real into the transcendental in the inviolate womb (Ries, 1991). 'I am that I am' carries within itself the mystery of every becoming. The light that enters into Zarathustra's grandmother, and later into Zarathustra's mother at the time of his conception, is incombustible. Moses, at the time of his spiritual awakening, is faced by a bush that burns without need of fuel (The Russian Orthodox Church identifies this bush with the mother of Jesus). The deity, as *causa sui*, speaks from this bush–womb in self-sufficiency.[5] 'I am that I am' is the voice of a sibling, of a baby that speaks from within the breast. Increate light is a means of orientation. But in asking the question, where is the centre? – it also knows how

---

[5] 'I am that I am.' Does Being when it has this form reveal a fundamental meaning to Becoming?

to bring about a ceasing to any orientation. The voice that speaks from among the angelic flames is the voice of increate light associated with a sibling. It would modulate the voices by means of which creationism would seem to have been a form of self-validation.[6]

A meaning fundamental to understanding Zoroaster's encounter with the gods of endless light is the fact that he collected soma (an undefined substance) and possibly a specific type of water, presumably in preparation for an act of sacrifice. There appears to be a relation between moments of visionary intensity and the meaning of the sacrifice, like the forming of increate light into the presence of gods. I turn in another direction. The Taoism of the *Tao Te Ching*, less threatened by the significance of darkness, is also less confrontational. It draws from sources that are different from the sources of Zoroastrianism.

> In Zoroastrianism, the principle of Darkness is essentially evil, while the principle of Light is essentially good. The fundamental conception of *yin* and *yang* is differ-

---

[6] Sergius Bulgakov, a revered figure among the theologians of the Russian Orthodox Church, has proposed rhapsodically a Mariolatry that he believes to inform all the sacred texts. 'The Old Testament speaks about the Mother of God [...] beginning with the very creation of the world which, according to the interpretation of St John of Damascus, prefigured the birth of the Most Holy Virgin. She is the new earth and heaven, created in place of the former ones defiled by sin. She is paradise and the woman promised by God in paradise, whose seed would trample the head of the serpent (Gen 3.15). She is Noah's Ark of salvation and the ladder seen in the dream of Jacob, she is the burning bush, seen by Moses, and the Red Sea in which Israel was saved. She is the tabernacle and the temple, in whole and in part... (Bulgakov, 1926: 117). The glory of God embraces in itself both the eternal world and the world created according to its image. In their ontological unity, Divine Sophia, which is revealed in the Son of Man (Bulgakov, 1926: 127).

ent. They are two interdependent and complementary facets of existence, and the aim of the *yin–yang* philosophers was not the triumph of light, but the attainment in human life of perfect balance between the two principles.

[WALEY, 1958: 112]

The Taoist sees a world consisting of the things for which language has no names. Provisionally we may call them *miao*, 'secret essence'. The world as seen in vision has no name. We can call it the sameness or the mystery. These names are however stop-gaps. For what we are trying to express is darker than any mystery.

[*IBID.*: 142]

And yet the meaning of the names is similar to the visions of Moses. 'Darkly visible, it (the Way) only seems as if it were there. ... It is indistinct and shadowy and yet within it there is an image' (*Tao Te Ching*, Lau, 1963, VI, XXI). The Way, in being 'darkly visible', is similar to the conflict in meaning that St ps.-Dionysius ascribes to God in thinking of him as 'a ray of darkness'. At least one gnostic myth assumes that universal darkness creates traces of light as a means to lead human beings into error.

It is the time of the London Blitz. A fireball grows at the end of a street; it becomes immense. A small, physically damaged child steps out of the fireball and moves down the street. 'What had seemed impossible and therefore unreal was now a fact and clear to them all. A figure had condensed out of the shuddering backdrop of the glare'

[WILLIAM GOLDING, 1979: 13]

The narrative of the Annunciation could be model for William Golding's astonishing description of being born out of an immense ball of increate light. The appearance of the fireball points to a moment when the logos as a ray of increate light, in entering the inviolate womb, reveals in space an absence that is more present than any presence (as a way of thinking about the origination of the Christ child). In terms of a psychoanalytic understanding, the narrative describes an eruption of increate light as indicating a coming together of the good objects and the extraordinary potency of the generative in acts of generation. In terms of a family, the unconscious good objects signify the coming together of a mother and father as the presence of a shared creativity. In this particular narrative, the coming together of a child and a mother reproduces in its potential creativity the coming together of the mother and father.

What is this thing of which you speak?
The thing, I said, that you call light.

[PLATO, *REPUBLIC* 507E]

If the seekers are searching for beauty, then why wait for the
hidden to be revealed? They should be startled and dazed by
the light emanating from the veil.

[MAULANA ABUL KALAM AZAD (IN JAMAL, 2010: XXIV)]

The radiance of beauty is distanced from any understanding, or from any undergoing, or from that which has been undergone. There is no immediate connection to events in time and space or to notions related to experience.[1] In ways of thinking reminiscent of Plato, a spiritual source to the generative that cannot be approached by epistemological means announces a dimension in which forms exist that the spirit is reluctant to accept. I imagine the remarkable Sūfi mystic and philosopher Shahab al-din-Suhrawardi (1154–1191) in the desert contemplating a vision of planets and stars in a radiant night sky and being overwhelmed by a sense of the transcendent. His book, *The Philosophy of*

---

[1] "[...] every moment I have lived, the world has been taking on light and fire for me, until has come to envelop me in one mass of luminosity, glowing from within. [...]" (Teilhard de Chardin, 1968: 13).

Illumination, translates the forms of a Platonic imagination into unworldly images of the luminous.

> If there is pure light, it cannot be pointed to, nor be located in body, nor have spatial dimensions.
>
> [AL-DIN-SUHRAWARDI (IN WALBRIDGE & ZIAI, 1999: 79)]

> If you wish to have a rule regarding light, let it be a light in its own reality. A sound mind will judge that the wisdom of the world of light, and the subtle order and astonishing correspondences occurring therein, to be greater than that of the world of darkness, which is but a shadow of the world of light. [*This sounds like a development of Zoroastrian ideas.*] That there are dominating lights, that the Creator of all is a light, that the archetypes are among the dominating lights, the pure souls have often beheld this to be so when they have detached themselves from their bodily temples. They then seek proof of it in others. All those possessing insight and detachment bear witness to this. [...] Plato, Socrates before him, and many of those before Socrates, held this view. Most said plainly that they had seen it in the world of light. The sages of Persia and India without exception agreed upon this.
>
> [*IBID.*: 107–108]

> Plato said: 'When freed from my body I beheld luminous spheres.' [...] Plato and his companions showed plainly that they believed the Maker of the universe and the world of intellect (*Nous*) to be light when he said that pure light is a world of intellect. Of himself, Plato said that in certain of his spiritual conditions he would shed his body and become free of matter. Then he would see light and splendour within his essence. He would ascend

to that all-encompassing divine cause and would seem to be located and suspended in it, beholding a mighty light in that lofty and divine place. But thought veiled that light from me.

[*IBID.*: 110]

Beauty disappears into a light that is without definition; no one can know its source. The poet, in seeing this beauty as a face, perceives a radiance un-contoured from which poetry can take on being. And yet the poem in forming also may be disinforming and disappear. The idea of a nothing that is palpable can be overwhelming. An effulgence that no eye can tolerate may form out of the coming together of the parental figures known as the good objects: this would be a way of thinking about the existence of a light of the mind, which may present itself as unlike any other experience. It just is as an existent. A contemplative mind may find a companion in this insight. Initially, the idea of measure is helpful: and yet it can lead to an unmarked boundary that bars further progress. The light of the mind, in so far as it is increate, is without context; it is set apart from creationist assumption; and it may have a relation to the unknowable that cannot be thought about. A Platonic experience of beauty, the timeless within time, is without a beginning or an end. Subject and object as modes of communication are no longer relevant. Epistemological theories are voided of meaning; dismay enters the instruments of measure; maps and timetables no longer record a knowable world.

Within the light, beauty can disappear. Or it can translate into an idea of justice as an idea that reflects beauty from a different point of view. Virtue, by being virtue, is able to insist on being acknowledged within the aura of beauty.

> It sees without seeing. It is most of all then that it sees. For then it sees light. And the other things that it saw were light-like in their form, though they were not light. […] It is actually in this way that Intelligence (*Nous*), covering its eyes so that it does not see other things, and collecting itself into its interior, and not looking at anything, will see a light that is not other than it or in another, but itself by itself alone and pure, and it appears to it all of a sudden, so that it is in doubt as to where it appeared from, outside or inside, and when it goes away it says, 'so it was inside – but again, not inside'.
>
> [PLOTINUS, *ENNEAD* 5.5.7]

> In fact, one must not try to discover where it comes from. For there is no 'anywhere'. It neither comes from nor goes anywhere, it both appears and does not appear. For this reason, it is necessary not to pursue it, but to remain in stillness, until it should appear, preparing oneself to be a contemplator.
>
> [*IBID.*: 5.5.8]

There is no depth and no shadow in the icon for it is pure givenness: 'The icon painter paints being that is given but in light; shadow is the absence of being.' The icon-painting depicts things as if they were made of light and not just reflect it. 'A metaphysics of light is the key feature of icon-painting.' It is at this point that Pavel Florensky proclaims himself to be a Platonist. From his perspective, it was Plato who understood light. All is light, he said. And light is what makes the face.

[KOZIN, 2007: 306²]

Images of the sacred in a biblical context can communicate intuitions concerning beauty and light.

> He has a form for the sake of his first and unique beauty, and all the limbs are not for use. For he does not have eyes for the purpose of seeing with them, for he sees from every side. His body is brighter than the visual spirit in us and more brilliant than any light; compared to him the light of the sun would be held in darkness. [...] He has the most beautiful form for the sake of man, in order that the pure in heart shall be able to see him, and they shall rejoice on account of whatever they have endured. For God has stamped man with his greatest seal, with his own form, in order that he shall rule and be lord over all things. And all things should serve him. For this reason, he who having judged that he is all and man his image – he being invisible and man as his image visible – will honour the image, which is man.

[PSEUDO-CLEMENTINE HOMILIES, THIRD CENTURY CE]

A rabbinical text reports that: 'A man's wisdom lights up a man's face. This means that his beauty lights up his face' (in Aaron, 1997). 'The apple of Adam's heel outshone the globe of the sun; how much more the brightness of his face' (*Midrash Rabba*).

There are metaphors in the words of the Ancients. They did not deny that predicates are mental and that

---

² The quotations are from a celebrated theoretician and monk, Pavel Florensky.

universals are in the mind; but when they said, 'There is a universal man in the world of the intellect', they meant that there is a dominating light containing different interacting rays whose shadow among magnitudes has the form of man. It is a universal – not in the sense that it is predicate, but in the sense that it has the same relation to the emancipation as to these individuals. It is as though it were the totality and the principle. This universal is not that universal whose conception does not preclude being shared; for they believe that it has a particularized essence and that it knows its essence.

[AL-DIN-SUHRAWARDI (IN WALBRIDGE & ZIAI, 1999: 109)]

The form of the visible is created by the invisible lines and paths of divine light.

[FLORENSKY, 1996: 128]

In this light 'we live, move and have our being.' It is the space of true reality.

[*IBID.*: 136–137]

Nothing need be negated for something to be uniquely individual. There is nothing to negate for until a thing is formed by light it has no existence whatsoever.

[*IBID.*: 145]

The patterns of the heavens were transmitted into the divine works of early artists.

[*IBID.*: 137]

In Islamic mysticism no text is more venerated than the Sura-al-Nur of Qur'an 24: 35. It provides a context for increate light.

> God is the light of the heavens and the earth. The symbol of his light is like a niche where there is a lamp. The lamp is in a glass. The glass is like a brilliant star. It is lit by a blessed olive tree, which is unrelated to the east or west, which the olive tree lights, even if no fire touches it.
>
> [SURA-AL-NUR OF QUR'AN 24: 35]

A radiance that is not of this world enables an inhabitant of this world to intuit a transcendental existence.

Islam in India. Among the Mogul emperors:

> Sufi saints including Mu'in a-Din had achieved *fana'* (annihilation), experiencing visions of God's brilliant light. Even Akbar upon hearing 'two heart-ravishing stanzas' of *quawwali* in 1578 saw flashes of divine lights; in the same year he had another mystic experience which Abu al-Fazl was to call the 'ecstasy of vision'. The authority for perceiving God as light commences with the famous Sura-al-Nur of the Qur'an, that is the chapter entitled Light.
>
> [ASHER, 2004: 163]

The extensive use of white marble on the Taj Mahal must have been intended to evoke a sense of divine presence, for light constantly changes and plays against the glistening surface.

[*IBID.*, 2004: 187]

Investing form with lucid stillness
Turning shadow into transient beauty
With slow rotation suggesting permanence.

[T. S. ELIOT, *BURNT NORTON*]

If the eye did not partake of the sun
How would it gaze on the light?
If we did not share in the power of God
In the godly we would not delight.

Goethe paraphrases Plotinus and ultimately Plato. [...]
In the same context, Goethe writes, 'The light calls for
an organ of the body that resembles itself and so the eye
was made by the light for the light, in order that the inner
light might face the outer light' [Goethe, *Collected Works*
XIII, 323]. As creatures of the light, the living creatures
are described in the new solar (Egyptian) theology as 'all
faces' or 'all eyes'.

[ASSMANN, 1995: 87]

Eye was formed by light, of light and for light, so that the
inner light might come into context with the outer light.

[GOETHE, *SCIENTIFIC STUDIES* (QUOTED IN CORBIN, 1994: 139)]

In thy light we shall see light.

[PSALM 35.10]

Father Seraphim: *"Why do you not look at me?"*

"I cannot look. Lightning flames from your eyes. Your face is brighter than the sun, and my eyes ache in pain."

"Fear not my son, you have become as bright as I am. You too are now in the fullness of God's spirit, otherwise you would not have been able to look at me as I am."

[MEYENDORFF, 1959: 161]

The Logos of God chose to manifest the true light of creation through his own flesh.

[ST. DIADOCHOS OF PHOTIKI, *PHILOKALIA* 1: 281)]

The intellect becomes so translucent that it sees its own light vividly when the divine light begins strongly to energise it.

[*IBID.*: 265]

Whoever partakes of divine illumination [...] to a proportionate degree possesses a spiritual knowledge of created things. [...] Through the fall, our nature was stripped of this divine illumination: but the logos of God had pity upon our disfigurement. In His compassion he took our nature upon himself, and on Mount Tabor He manifested it to his disciples clothed once again most brilliantly. [...] Adam before the fall also participated in this divine illumination

and resplendence; and because he was truly clothed in a
garment of glory, he was not naked.

[ST GREGORY PALAMAS, *PHILOKALIA* 4: 375]

At midnight on the Emperor's pavement flit
Flames that no faggot feeds, nor steel has lit,
Nor storm disturbs, flames begotten of flame,
Where blood-begotten spirits come
And all complexities of fury leave,
Dying into a dance,
An agony of trance,
An agony of flame that cannot singe a sleeve.

[W. B. YEATS, *BYZANTIUM*]

The Lord went before them in a pillar of cloud by day to guide
them along the way and in a pillar of fire by night to give them
light, so that they might travel day and night. The pillar of
cloud by day and the pillar of fire did not depart from before
the people.

[EXODUS 13:20]

The god soars upwards in an unbounded pillar of increate light. 'If the light of a thousand suns were to blaze forth all at once in the sky, they might resemble the splendour of this exalted being' (*Bhagavad Gita*: 139).[1] Like a Hindu temple, the pillar is flanked by extraordinary carvings.[2] Adam before

---

[1] Walter Hilton, in *The Ladder of Perfection* (1957: 2.32), describes Christ as sitting in a bodily light as great as a thousand suns (cf. Minnis, 1983: 364). One of the ways in which increate light differs from natural light is in its other-worldly intensity. It is so intense that it may appear to the human eye as darkness visible.

[2] Compare 'The fallen phallus of Rudra (Shiva), transfigured as a cosmic phallic pillar, flamed upwards from the netherworld into the heavens. [...] It rose in cosmic

the fall conveys a similar sense of being a bodily infinite. At the beginning reputedly he was greater in size than any giant and unbounded in radiance.[3]

Marianne Moore has described the desert as a 'translucent mistake', which would be a way of thinking about the wilderness that the Israelites had to travel through over many years.[4] And yet here, where absence can present itself as a formidable antagonist, the visionary is more in evidence than in any other place: here Elijah speaks with ravens, and the immeasurable inspires a prophet. In this space, the becoming of the contemplative may yield up a token of itself. A pillar of fire that binds sky to earth and a cloud with a floating tail that almost touches the ground guide the Israelites through the desert. (The cloud is dark with rain by day and radiant with light by night.) A similar cloud – or it may be the same cloud as a shadow of the cosmos – harbours Moses for forty days and forty nights. Within it, Moses meditates, as though allowed entrance into God's mind. A similar cloud in association with increate light appears in the narrative of the Transfiguration as a womb-like setting for the deity himself. St Gregory Palamas thinks of this particular moment of illumination as a basis for religious insight. Moses, Elijah and

night in terrible splendour from immeasurable depths' (Kramrisch, *The Presence of Shiva*. 1981: 159; quoted by Muller-Ortega, 2004). In this aspect Shiva defeats Brahma and Vishnu.

[3] In Sūfi belief the original Adam was Phos (which means light). 'Phos, innocent and peaceful, pre-existed in paradise. The Archons tricked him into clothing himself in the corporeal Adam' (Corbin, *The Man of Light in Iranian Sufism*, 1994: 15).

[4] In "Abundance", the second part of a multiple poem called *The Jeraboa* (in White, 2017: 103).

Jesus rise into the sky, in a conception of space disavowed by space travel and yet meaningful in vision. Increate light touches the sleeve of the Son as though in recall of the act by which he was engendered. It is as though innately each of us was a receptor of such a light. The founding of the first tabernacle is from such a vision of glory. The guiding pillar of fire, evident at Mount Sinai, rests over the Tabernacle and spears within it as a guidance and protection. Cf. *Numbers*, 14:14 'Thou goest before them by daytime in a pillar of a cloud and in a pillar of fire by night.' […] The cloud is God's vehicle, while the fire is his glory or increate light: compare 24:17, 'the appearance of God's glory was like a consuming fire' (*Numbers* 9: 15–23).[5] God's fiery presence rests a cloud on the roof of the tabernacle.

A divine element may begin to manifest itself through acts of contemplation, and the insights of Bion and of Trouillard into the nature of contemplation may begin to release their meaning. The generosity in innocence of the virgin's womb activates transformation. Agents of the Holy Spirit, celestial tongues of fire rather than pillars or clouds associated with fire, make sacred imprints upon the earth as footsteps in the memory. Cathedrals, often visionary anticipations of the real, give shape and time to intuitions of unknowable source. Sacrality informs the meaning of the labyrinth carved into the stone floor of Chartres cathedral, which reflects the shape

---

[5] 'He made darkness his hiding place. About him was his tabernacle, dark water in clouds of air' (Psalm 18:11).

of the rose window above it as though it were a pilgrim's mandala. The encounter of increate light and creativity is not accidental. Shy, timid Moses has no hesitation in plunging into the womb-cloud,

> into the truly mysterious darkness of unknowing. Here, renouncing all that the mind may conceive, wrapped entirely in the intangible and invisible, he belongs completely to him who is beyond everything.
>
> [ST PS.-DIONYSIUS, *THE MYSTICAL THEOLOGY* (IN LUIBHEID, 1987: 137)]

The cloud of glory/increate light is the cloud of unknowing of fourteenth-century English mysticism.

> The more we take flight upward, the more our words are confined to the ideas we are capable of forming; so that now, as we plunge into the darkness that is beyond intellect, we shall find ourselves not simply running short of words but actually speechless and unknowing.
>
> [*IBID.*: 139]

> The more my argument climbs, the more language falters, and when it has passed beyond the ascent, it will turn silent completely, since it will finally be at one with Him who is indescribable.
>
> [*IBID.*: 139]

Urgency quickens the steps of the prophet. The barren spaces that promised death enable him to discover an association of increate light with the tongues of angels in a bush that burns without need of sustenance. One of the three

Cappadocian brothers, Gregory Nazianzius, was to assume that the cloud was a form of deterrent, while his brother, Gregory of Nyssa, assumed it to be a self-contradicting idea in the form of a revelation (Bady, 2013: 468).

> Our initial withdrawal from wrong and erroneous ideas concerning God is by way of a transition from darkness to light. An awareness of hidden things guides the soul through sense phenomena to a world of the invisible. The awareness is a kind of cloud, which overshadows all appearances, and slowly guides and accustoms the soul to look towards what is hidden. As she leaves below all that human nature can attain, the soul enters into the secret chamber of divine knowledge, and here she is cut off on all sides by the divine darkness. Now she leaves behind her all that can be grasped by sense or reason, and all that is left for her contemplation is the invisible and the incomprehensible.
>
> [GREGORY OF NYSSA. SERMON 11 (IN DANIÉLOU, 1962: 247)]

Is this the most helpful way of defining the relation of 'O' to states of psychological 'becoming'?

> Cloud and light in a sense correspond to the primal antithesis of dark and light (*Genesis*, 12–13). Cloud becomes visible by negating the daylight and fire dispels the night. In another sense, cloud and fire are complementary, since the word used for cloud is a word used for smoke (and the Israelites considered lightning to be a form of combustion).
>
> [PROPP, 1999: 549–550]

That which lies between place and its absence may present itself as a symbol without a history; it can appear and disappear without any meaningful relation to the other.

> In Sūfi thought, God creates man in his own image. Since man cannot know God, he must in defining himself reflect a mystery. But there is an intermediary: the Imagination, or the Cloud of visionary understanding
> [CORBIN, 1958]

A widespread belief in incarnation as a pre-ordained fact (see Bucur, 2008) does not require a creationist model to validate its existence. The mystery of the Incarnation must baffle any attempt to realise its meaning in thought (Bady, 2013).[6] Aryeh Wineman has discovered in Hasidic belief an understanding of increate light, which God denied to human kind as a way of punishing our first parents.

M. R. James (2004), in his collection of the Apocrypha, includes a sixth-century Syriac legend of wide-spread influence, in which a royal family send their son to Egypt to seize a certain pearl from a dragon. In Egypt the young man is captured, imprisoned in a well and forced to eat the food

---

[6] 'Medieval theorists developed their understandings of ecstatic vision in both exegetical and devotional contexts. The first biblical visionary turns out to have been, surprisingly, Adam. Western exegetes were familiar with a version of Gen.2. 21 based on the Septuagint, in which the "deep sleep" (Hebrew *tardema*) that God sends upon Adam is not *sopor* as in the Vulgate, but *exstasis*. On this reading, the entranced Adam's soul ascended to heaven and learned from the angels while God was creating Eve, so that on his return he prophesied not only their marital union but also the union of Christ and the Church which it prefigured' (Newman, 2005: 10).

of forgetfulness.[7] The parents of the imprisoned prince send him a message that enables him to escape from the well and to seize the pearl from the dragon. On returning home, he is greeted as a hero and clothed in robes of light.[8] The loss of any truth in vision, represented by the food of forgetfulness and by the well in which darkness presents itself in layers, is 'the leitmotiv of Iranian spirituality', and it appears in at least one Sanskrit text (Corbin, 1994: 24). The darkness of the well in its powers of suppression is antithetical in meaning to the meaning of increate light.

> The material body of the one who has attained mystical experience is like a tunic. Sometimes he casts it off and at other times he puts it on. [...] He ascends towards the light at will. If it pleases him, he can manifest himself in whatever form he chooses. [...] When he has undergone the action of light and put on the robe of auroral Light, [he discovers that] the robe too is able to influence and

---

[7] The well of darkness sounds to me like a pessimistic Lockeian understanding of life in the womb. Presumably a Wordsworthian would relate life in the womb to an experience of light. I presume that the alternation of light and dark in foetal perception must be important in the experience of womb life. The concern with darkness and the presumed evil of matter has a Gnostic flavour about it.

[8] The Yezidi people now of Iraq, at one time possibly followers of Zoroaster, have a number of pearl myths that may or may not be relevant to the meaning of increate light in the Syriac legend. Among them is at least one creationist myth, in which a pearl identified with increate light is the source of the cosmos. There is universal darkness, and God identified with increate light creates a throne out of the pearl. 'In this ocean there was only a pearl. [...] You quickly gave it a soul, You made your own light manifest in it. [...] Did the pearl come from the king or the king from the pearl? [...] Let us praise the white pearl. A cup was created from it (*the inviolate womb, the chalice of the last supper?*). [...] There love had its place. [...] The pearl burst open in its awe. It no longer had the strength to contain God. Water came from the pearl. It became the ocean.' Some of the Zoroastrians went into India. It would be fascinating to know whether or not myths of origins concerning, for instance, the Vedic golden germ are related to them (Rodziewicz, 2016).

to act; it makes a sign, and the sign is obeyed; it imagines, and what it imagines comes to be accordingly. [...]
The perfected man, the man in love with harmony, is
immune from evil: he acts through the energy and with
the help of the Light because he himself is a child of the
world of Light

[AL-SUHRAWARDI, *BOOK OF CONVERSATIONS* (IN CORBIN, 1960)]

The dynamic of the Annunciation, the logos of increate light
as it informs the narrative of the Transfiguration, enables the
logos to touch with radiance the garments of the ascend-
ing Christ.[9] A ray of light brings into view that which was
powerfully present even when unseen. In the narrative of
the Transfiguration, Jesus enters a dual state: he is in prayer
before the mountain as well as being part of a prayerful
vision rising up from a mountain slope: a figure praying in
time is able to perceive itself in other forms of representation. 'His face shone like the sun and his clothes became
as white as the light' (*Matthew* 17). Jesus commands the
disciples to tell no one about the vision before his death and
resurrection (*Matthew* 17.9). Two of the disciples turn away
from the vision; it could be that they turn aside, by looking
earthwards, in order to understand the miracle in terms of
reverie or dream or prayer rather than in actuality. Or it
could be, as the gnostic *Pistis Sophia* suggests (Chapter 3),
that the human eye cannot bear the brilliance of this light.

---

[9] The transforming relation of increate light to material or other substances is like
an artist's transformation of a canvas surface by the use of paint.

Andrei Orlov and Alexander Golitzin have discovered a parallel between a Jewish apocalyptic text written in the first century C.E. and an account from a thousand years later concerning the practice of Hesychasm and the internalisation in parable of a presence that is thought to be 'out there'.

> It is apparent that the symbolism of these two descriptions belongs to different worlds. In the first one, an adept, on a celestial mission, finds himself before the glorious appearance of the Lord, accompanied by angels who extract him from his earthly garments and anoint him with delightful oil. In the second one, he is led through darkness and 'an impenetrable density' in an inner journey to the depths of his heart. The majesty of the celestial environment strikingly confronts the monotonous quietness of inner contemplation. [...] In both descriptions the visionaries see themselves as luminescent. The metamorphosis is total: both mystical adepts become 'entirely' luminous. [...] In the first account, the divine light comes from outside, from a glorious appearance of the Lord. In the second account, the illumination comes from inside, from a darkness of the soul, proceeding from the open space of the heart of the visionary.
>
> [ORLOV & GOLITZIN, 2001: 282][10]

Before the Fall, the radiance of Adam and Eve did not require the contour of a skin; they were radiant and

---

[10] There is another set of myths concerning Adam's lack of a backside and the near explosion of his bowels when someone feeds him a grain of wheat (instead of an apple?). God sends a little bird to peck out an anus for Adam, and all is well. But an apple a day keeps the doctor away: Eve's wisdom.

indefinable. Tunics of skin clothed them as a result of the Fall, and in ecstasy they could no longer know total penetration.

> Light was hidden in the sense that there was a change in consciousness. Adam and the generations following him were no longer capable of relating to the Light. As a consequence, humans could understand the sacred texts of the Torah only in terms of its black letters rather than by the evidence conveyed by its white space and non-black letters. They could read the Torah only in terms of physical actions, while being blind to its more experiential and spiritually sublime aspect, which is not visible by way of the letters of the Torah itself.
>
> [WINEMAN, 2019][11]

The relation of a background white space to the foreground black type is relevant to the meaning of certain poetry, as with Stephane Mallarmé's poem *Un coup de dés jamais n'abolira le hasard*, remarkable in its iconography, concerning the throw of a dice.

The light that brought brilliance to the garments that Jesus wore signified the unique identity in difference of the Trinity: with the Father and the Son in communion with each other in relation to increate light which in this context is the Holy Spirit. At one time, the whitening of garments in Aztec ritual signified a special relation between beings on earth and beings who were allowed access to the heavens.

---

[11] See also G. Scholem, 'The Meaning of the Torah in Jewish Mysticism' (1956).

The god Nanahuatl was covered in feather-down and diatomite (a whitening element) before he threw himself into a bonfire in order to be transformed into the Fifth Sun. After being consumed, he rose into the sky, where the primordial couple awaited him. [...] Prisoners of war destined for the sacrifice and adorned in a similar way shared the same celestial destination after death. They were deified as beings that rose daily into the sky, escorting the sun on its quotidian journey to the zenith. Rites involving victims so adorned were often aimed at recreating the principal event of Mesoamerican cosmology: the primordial appearance of light.

[DUPEY GARCÍA, 2015: 75]

The ascent of Christ correlates with the deity's speaking from inside a cloud.

The Aztecs conceived of clouds as beings who wear cotton clothing, based on the similarity between the appearance of meteorological phenomena and the texture and colour of this fibre. [...] Feather down was symbolic of clouds. [...] Since the human body was a model used to comprehend the cosmos in pre-Columbian ideology, it makes sense to call the clouds the 'sky's attire'.

[IBID.: 78]

It was thought that 'bearers of the whitening element, women in childbirth, would metamorphose into clouds if they should die'.

[IBID.: 79]

67

Prajâpati: *The âtmàn is when one is fast asleep, totally collected and serene, and without dreams – that is the immortal self. It is free from fear in its relation to the Brahman or Absolute.*

[CHANDOGYA UPANISHAD 11.1]

The Brahman is self-luminous; it is the light of lights.

[BRAHMA SUTRAS: 95]

[In Shankaracharya's commentary,] 'It is the principle of intelligence, and it shines before everything else.'

[IBID.]

He dreams by means of his own radiance. He dreams with his own light. He becomes his own light.

[BRHADARANYCHA UPANISHAD 4.3.9]

Before Adam's fall, the relation of increate light to created being was one of enablement. In my paradigm concerning the Annunciation narrative, a ray of increate light releases the possibility of a sacred birth from among the created, on condition that the place of engenderment should be inaccessible to anyone or anything else. Almost in parallel, but much later, tongues of fire in descent through a night sky release the radiance of acts of creative making in places otherwise dull in their interest. Alternations between increate light and the created are complicated in so far as they involve an apophatic process: one dimension must enter a process of becoming the unknowable if another dimension is to be made knowable; in effect, creation in its many ways of communicating must disappear if a vision of increate light is to appear. Moses within the cloud of unknowing must engage with spiritual and life-risking turbulence to arrive at a vision of increate light. Transformations of this kind can operate by means of reversals in movement. The vision of increate light disappears as I recover creation and its ways of being articulate. The transformations are reminiscent of thematic transformation in music.

The book of Genesis does not practise transformations in this way. Its God speaks, and a cosmos puts itself forward in conditions of time that are not those of vision. The logos of God is absolute. There is no indicating of a relation between the increate and the created. I believe that the absence is evidence of a disablement (to give one example), as in the case of the Tower of Babel story, a retelling of a creationist story (and its relation to language) that is open about the inadequacy of a creationism that has no relation to the idea of increate light. Genesis is too restricted as a spiritual model; in a sense, it is too sure of itself. Exodus is otherwise; there is a sense of regret as well of as of visionary suffering; the ground is forever slipping beneath the feet of the reluctant traveller; the absence of an *oikonomia* marks the beginning of vision. In transformations of this kind, the uses of language will always appear strange.[1] Not everyone would agree to this model for thought.

> Breath is intelligence and intelligence is breath. When a man is fast asleep and sees no dreams at all, then these become unified within this very breath. His speech then merges into it together with all the names; his sight merges into it together with all the visible appearances; his hearing merges into it together with all the sounds; and his mind merges into it together with all his thoughts. And when he awakes, these fly off – as from a blazing fire sparks fly off in every direction, so from this self the vital functions fly off to their respective stations, and from the vital functions the gods, and from the gods, the worlds.
>
> [KAUSHITAKI UPANISHAD 111.3]

> [It] is the True, the real, the Self, whose nature is pure intelligence [...] lifts itself above the vain conceit of being one with this body, and itself becomes the Self, whose nature is unchanging eternal cognition, as such scriptural passages declare as 'He who knows the highest Brahman becomes even Brahman.'
>
> [MUNDYAKA UPANISHAD III.II.9]

> Before the rise of discriminative knowledge *the nature of the individual self, which is (in reality) pure light* [my italics], is non-discriminated as it were from its limiting

---

[1] Spirituality in Genesis and spirituality in Exodus are dissimilar; and they are so to an extent that they are able to disclose a dualism in the spiritual. In Genesis, spirituality is as unselfconscious as an act of physical digestion; it is something that is passed through and appears unrelated to any idea of termination. In Exodus it takes on the depth that is always apparent if introspection is bound up with regret. Moses' experience of the apophatic is inseparable from being an act of mourning. A move forward of the spirit carries within it a retreating sense of sorrow.

adjuncts consisting of body, senses, mind, sense objects
and feelings.

[SHANKARA'S COMMENTARY ON THE BRAHMA SUTRA 1.III.19
(IN RADHAKRISHNAN & MOORE, 1973: 515)]

The idea that I might engage with increate light by way of
an ecstatic identification has quite a different prospectus in
early Indian thought. Increate light exists everywhere; but
it exists in relation to an imagination that changes the angle
as it turns about it. Among the seers devoted to a religious
life, the remarkable Sri Shankaracharya – who lived c.800
C.E. – proposed an interpretation of the Upanishads and of
other Vedic texts, some of them dating to hundreds of years
before the common era, that overrides any presumption that
spiritual insight and acts of knowing might be enabling of
each other; there is no effective relation between increate
light and the belief that knowledge might have a truthful
form. In fact, spiritual identifications of any kind are iso-
lated from theories of knowledge. Creation as an existent
is an illusion rather than a failure; it has the form of being
the veil of deceit known as Maya; and only in deepest sleep,
when there is no consciousness of self, can selfhood be separated from Maya; at which time an aspect of the self, known
as the âtmàn, is able to achieve in an unknowable ecstasy an
identification with increate light, which on this occasion has
the form of being the Brahman. The apophatic as a potent
point of transmission between creation and the increate
has no place in this means of perception. Truth exists in

an unknowable identification that is associated with the deepest sleep, in which consciousness is not present; it is thought that all transformations in the world, including the states of perception associated with dream and reverie, are forms of deception.

Sri Shankaracharya points out that many of the Upanishad texts give no evidence that knowing might be related to an identification with increate light. Ecstasy, as a condition for there being such an identification, is a state of renewal; it is not a form of knowledge; and indeed, it exists in opposition to any realisation of knowledge. To live in circumstances that idealise learning and knowledge is to promote self-deception. It is to elicit the veils of untruth.[2]

If you said that dreaming might provide a key to insight, I would agree with you; but why should deepest sleep with its apparent absence of anything related to a world of light, and yet as the source of an identification with increate light, grant access to such a key?

A self at the centre of its own world is able to control (or at least to think that it controls) the concepts within its ability

---

[2] Commentators on the writings of Plotinus have recognised that there is an absence of reconciliation between Plotinus' theories concerning a moving towards One and a mystical union with the One that may follow and, in a contrary movement, having the world of forms separate from the One so that the world shows itself to be in its unfolding a mysterious conduit for meaning that flows outwards (or downwards) from the immense energies of the One. Sri Shankaracharya describes a union not unlike Plotinus' mystic union with the One, but his Upanishad perceptions do not allow him to demonstrate that the Brahman might be the source of a world that is other than delusional. A follower of Plotinus legitimately might take delight in the beauty of the world, while a follower of Sri Shankaracharya will think that any such perception of beauty is one of Maya's deceptions.

to think. If I posit this imaginary centre as being outside the self, then any means of communication that the self might be able to have access to reveals itself potentially to be under the threat of a retreat into the apophatic. So far as I know, the Upanishads provide no such view. The abiding nature of the ecstatic primal relationship is revived every time I enter deepest sleep; while the exercise of experience, whether in daily life or in dreaming, both being deceptions, is like a stone thrown into a dark pool that disappears into darkness as the pool returns to stillness. I move from a kingdom of the deceptive, over which the self thinks itself to be sovereign, to an unknowable acquirement of relation to increate light. The Absolute sustains a link without involving itself in the evidential, and when dreaming has retreated from any play in mind. This fundamental relationship of an aspect of self-hood with the Brahman or increate light might be a way of defining the 'becoming' of Bion or Trouillard; but about this I am not certain.

There are two positions, and in between them language appears as an instrument of creation that is secure in defini-tion so long as it is part of an interchange. The definition is lost if the language should show itself to be correlated with the appearances and disappearances of increate light – and when the apophatic has become operational. In *Burnt Nor-ton*, the first of his *Four Quartets*, T. S. Eliot considers states of verbal incoherence ('Words strain, crack, and sometimes break …'). I assume that he is writing about a journey into the apophatic when indeed everything can fall apart, although his conscious intention may have been to express an anxious scruple. The problem is one that concerns the meaning of a certain spiritual circumstance; it is not too distant from the circumstance in which Moses meditated on the significance of spiritual law.

The closest that I have come to an awareness of an apophatic experience came to me long after the time of my having had the experience. The concept of 'beginning' is central to it and by means of this concept it is relatable to the Genesis creation and to the vision of Christ as increate light in the Prelude to the Gospel according to St John, in which Christ is associated with a mysteriously deep understanding of 'beginning'.[3] The concept is unsecured; its slips and slides as though its guise as a beginning was one of deception. Everything wavers, as though on a point of disappearance. If I stretch out towards the concept, I find that it recedes.

My almost physical reaction to this meaning marked the onset of an apophatic crisis that I was unable to recognise. I was travelling with members of my family through the dark of a prehistoric cave in France. The vehicle we were in came to a stop. Before us were marks on a wall, uncertainly related

---

[3] In the beginning was the Word, and the Word was with God, and the word was God.

The same was in the beginning with God.

All things were made by him; and without him was not anything made that was made.

In him was life; and the life was the light of men.

And the light shineth in darkness; and the darkness comprehended it not.

[The Gospel according to St John 1:1]

to shade and light as they intimated the shapes of animals. Being seemed to be about to emerge out of a state of non being.[4] Intuitions of the unexpected – and yet also of the familiar – entered the moment. I desired to stretch out and touch the marks: the intensity of the urge being close to irresistible. It is as though by means of a movement a hand could cross millennia into a past that was temporally of incalculable distance from me; as though all time were contained in the deceptive idea of a 'beginning'. I held back; I did not stretch out my hand; the sense of prohibition was more powerful than the impulse to reach out. I was a creature living in time. Something other than a conscious self had restrained me. I now think of a world long ended; and of the model of a mammoth outside another cave that was mechanically geared to shudder and periodically to roar, a deeply saddening object, a life lost in a world of unlived or un-survived lives, as an aspect of living in time.

In my thinking now about this apophatic experience, I find that what remains with me is how the disabling of language in relation to models of creation in this case initially took the form of doubts about any steady meanings concerning 'beginning' when the concept was unloosed in revelation from the measures of time and space. The radiance that enables Christ to manifest himself in the world will in time take him out of human sight; and language, and the models

---

[4] Perceptions of a past creation were like intimations of a future creation, as though God were holding out his hand.

of creation on which language depends, will then stabilise on return.

In the Advaita Vedanta increate light is the sole truth, and all evidence of subject and object must be lost in any ecstasy. It is possible that mind has no means to pursue this insight: there is a sense of contraction or expansion, intimations of an indefinable that press in on the contemplating mind, as though the indefinable were seeking to form into definitions. If I assume that symbols are forms of self-extension, and so validated by an ascription of a certain sovereignty to the self, then the apophatic as an issue can be set aside. Only if I see thought as a derivative of increate light by way of an apophatic transformation will I find that my means of communication have become incoherent. In relation to increate light, Moses was at a loss for words in finding that words had deserted him. The increate light of deepest sleep may be able to define me, but how am I to define my relation to it? Any psychology that depends on unknowing for insight must be weird; and yet I am very attracted to an idea of the apophatic. Even so, when I read Louis Renou's description of the âtmàn aspect to the enquiring soul, I find it hard to understand how this understanding of personality might be part of a coherent psychology.

> Since the Rig-Veda, the word âtmàn has denoted something that is at the base of the animated character of living beings (or, what comes to the same thing from the Vedic point of view, of beings which are inert but

are conceived of as living). It is akin to two terms, both rare in the ancient portions of the Rig-Veda: *prana* and *asu*. *Prana* and *asu* are vital breath, *prana* in the physiological sense; *asu* in clear connection with death and the beyond and at times approaching the notion of psyche. [...] From the beginning it could designate a person. [...] In the Artharva-veda the association of âtmàn with wind or breath tends to disappear, and the âtmàn is represented as distinct from breath. The expression *itaram armanam* denotes 'the remaining part of the human being, when eye and breath have been separated, namely the âtmàn'. [...] Âtmàn as person is distinguished from exterior appurtenances: either from the series father, son, wife, or from the series cattle or cows. [...] Its dominant use is as a reflexive pronoun connected with the meaning of person. [...] In the Agnicayana ceremony, we find the altar identified with the body (âtmàn) of the sacrificer; and as the sacrificer is none other than Prajâpati, âtmàn denotes at the same time the ritualistic personality reconstructed by the sacrifice (*ibid.*, 155). Âtmàn is the trunk of the altar in contrast with its tail or wings. Here the âtmàn is solid like a body. But elsewhere it is thought to be immaterial. [...] In the Brahmanas, it is not the body, nor the person, nor the soul, nor the breath; it participates in all these elements. It completes a given element, as the whole completes the parts. If you take the limbs, it will be the trunk, if you take the body it will be the entire person. It is added to the person to confer on him life or divine individuality, always going from the human plane to the sacrificial one, from this again to the divine one. It is always a construction or the result of

a construction. [...] In the Upanishads, it is an absolute
that confers consciousness and wisdom on all beings.

[RENOU, 1952]

To enter into the apophatic is to enter into a movement in
which to move in any direction is to lose any relation to
communication and to any of the creationist models on
which the means of communication depend. I enter the
cloud of glory that is the cloud of unknowing as a site where
visions of the increate are conceivable. I move in a direction
in which definitions of any kind, including any attempt to
define psychology, must be marginalised (as when I try to
define the psychology of the one who makes the apophatic
journey in terms of the âtmàn). I do not know whether
or not these issues apply if the point of departure and the
extended direction is from increate light as the Absolute
or Brahman, or from the radiation of selfhood as a kind of
pseudo-spirituality. The truth is that I have no insight in
regard to these issues, although I sense their importance.

It seems to me that the sages of old who wanted to attract to themselves the presence of the gods, and build temples and statues to that end, looking to the nature of the universe, had in mind that the nature of the soul is a thing that is in a general way easy to attract, but the easiest way of all to receive it would be if one were to craft something sympathetic which was able to receive some share of it. And that is sympathetic, which is in one way imitative of it, like a mirror able to capture some image of it.

[PLOTINUS, *ENNEAD*, 4.3.11]

In central India I pass a roadside place of worship that is more a shrine than a temple. The young Brahmin priest who welcomes me into this space is so thin and ethereal, I wonder whether he eats anything at all. Inside this sacred space, he draws a circle of light around an idol by moving the light (of a candle?) in a circular fashion before the presence of the idol, as though eliciting some truth from it. Later I came to the view that he was performing an act of *Darśan*[1]. By means of circling the light, he is able to control the direction in which the worshipper looks and at the same time by the same circular movement transform the meaning of the

---

[1] Diana L. Eck (1998), in her study of *Darśan*, describes the ceremony as *arati*. It is so central in importance to Hindu worship that it can replace the term for worship, which is *puja*.

perception so that the profane (the substance out of which the icon was made, as well as the un-informed glance) might be transformed into the sacred as an action in space. It would seem to me that controlling the perception of the observer and transforming the psychic level of understanding concerning the meaning of the object of perception are aspects of the same function.[2] I am now inclined to think that the meaning of the circling light is comparable to the meaning, first, of the ray of increate light that enters the virgin's womb and, second, to the circular significance of halos and aureoles as spaces associated with the celestial imagination and the meaning of realising a deity in a luminous circle.[3] The circling of the light is a way of perceiving logos.

Out of the substance of an idol, the Brahmin priest appeared to be transforming a material fact into a spiritual presence, as a presence no different in effect from the effect of light transforming an experience of a stained-glass window by passing through it. Magical transformations of this kind reflect on the value of acts of contemplation. A means of perception (looking into the circle of light) transposed into an object of perception is a transcendental meaning that takes

---

[2] Imagine Milton as looking into Galileo's 'optic glass' and as thinking the heavens improbably to be transformed as well as controlled by an instrument that would appear to control direction. If Milton had been able to peer through Galileo's telescope, he might have seen nothing: a different world nourished his imagination. Galileo, his contemporary, lived in a future that was closed to him.

[3] The issue of controlling perception in relation to the spiritual indicates to me that visions of increate light on a psychoanalytic level may have the significance of intrusions into the primal scene. People can go physically as well as spiritually blind through unconscious or conscious intrusions into the primal scene.

on the values of an imminent meaning. Conversely, a Hindu artist must find ways by which to draw the spiritual into the non-spiritual matière with which he works. In the creation of art – whether it be of an idol or of a site for acts of worship – the artist must find a way to enable a divine spirit (or multiple dimensions of this spirit) to enter the clay or metal or other substance that is called on in the making of idols or of sacred architectural structures.

Controlling a means of perception (as by means of circling a light) can signify an act of translation between physical and spiritual meanings. I find this dual action to be relevant to one of the points from which I started, which is Trouillard's perception that *to contemplate is to become*. The numinous significance of light circling around an idol is to generate or to restore. In my becoming, through an act of contemplation, I am enabling something other, over which I have no control, possibly to take on being as an act of becoming. There is a transaction between the here-and-now and the there-and-then. The process is two-way: either I release the spiritual from the physical presence (as occurs within the circle of light), or I release a physical presence from an oppressive physicality and enable it to become a spiritual emanation.

Plotinus believed that 'the sages of old [...] built temples and statues [...] to attract the presence of the gods to themselves' (*Ennead*, 4.3.11). The gods as a means of transmission are inseparable in meaning from the numinous significance of sunlight, as when sunlight is believed to be a type of numinous light. Mirrors catching the sun's reflection perform the same function, but to less sustained effect. The principle known as the logos (or the logoi) is similar as a conduit of meaning when it is used as means of transmission through interrupted passages. In the Prologue to the Gospel of St John, the idea of logos is inseparable from increate light as aspects of the redeemer. It is one of the meanings of increate light that it can be transmitted across boundaries that otherwise cannot be crossed – and so show itself to be the Wordsworth/Meltzer cloud of glory that attends an act of birth – as an act that has resulted as a renewal rather than as a death into life. The legend of the Annunciation describes a similar transformation. The sacred meaning of a certain ray of increate light, and a certain means of containing the ray in a conjunction that is generative, has an effect of re-validating the awesome and mysterious conjunction of ray and container. 'Virgin' in the concept of 'virgin womb' indicates the understanding that an otherworldly (and 'pure') meaning to the generative container is fundamental to the forming of its physical usefulness.

Increate light and its association to life itself came together in the thought of Plotinus.

> Light is no longer a mere physical accident, but a manifestation of the spiritual principle of reality and activity in the luminary, its logos or eidos. [...] It is the principle of form in the material world. It holds the position of form in relation to the other elements. [...] It has a special-

status (by being) on the frontiers of spirit and matter.
[…] It is a Platonic conception of reality as a hierarchy,
sensible and intelligible, through the mediation of a half-
spiritual, half-material realm of light.

[ARMSTRONG, 1937]

We move up to the One, carried on by a kind of wave,
when suddenly we see: not an object but light itself. Just
as there is no distinction between the intelligence and its
object, so here there is no distinction between the object
seen and the light that illuminates it: there is but light
(*Ennead* 6.7.38). […] Light is not considered to enable
vision, but is sight itself. […] There is no organ such as
the eye, and no looking outside the organ. Light is seen by
light: light sees itself […] the soul sees light itself which
is formless.

[MORLEY, 1975: 370–371]

One understanding of the relation between the contemplative and becoming would have becoming (as in a Brahmin priest's act of *Darśan*) determine the meaning of the
contemplative (identified with the spectator). Becoming,
as the consequence of a circular movement of increate
light, transforms the act of contemplation. Ghislain Casas
has pointed out in an article, 'Les statues vivent aussi:
Theorie néoplatonicienne de l'objet rituel' (2014), how the
late Neoplatonists who had turned to magic – they were
known as theurgists – believed that objects were divinely
inspired because the symbol as a generative resource
worked within them.

The objects in themselves and by themselves did not symbolise anything, this being once more a theory concerning procreation as an interiority to the sacred. In terms of this understanding, the Brahmin priest does not project sacrality into the profane object: rather, he releases sacrality from it. Proclus, in relation to this view, believed that ritual was a secret life inherent in things themselves (*ibid.*: 678) as a manner of turning towards a secret source, much as the heliotrope (i.e. the sunflower) turns and twists its stem towards the sun, or the selenotrope (wonderful word!) twists its stem in the direction of the path followed by the moon.]

The dynamics of the circling light and of the Annunciation legend have an absence be transformed into a presence (that of a god–man), that is analogous to the meaning of the Transfiguration legend. Increate light touches the garments of Jesus so that they radiate with light. (Much as, in Psalm 104, God is thought to cover himself with light 'as with a garment'.) In the Annunciation legend, an act of otherworldly creation requires a transcendental means of containment in order for an artisan who is angelic to enable an act of radical transformation to take place.[4] Semen as a material code is translated into the endowment of increate light. The nature of the womb, in its relation to virginity as an aspect of grace, is like the ritual transformation of clay and metal into spir-

---

[4] By my desk, as I work on this book, I have a National Gallery reproduction of a Fra Lippo Lippi's fresco/painting of the Annunciation. One of the meanings of the picture, which is immediate, is that the angel and young woman are in love with each other, and that this shows by way of their shyness and modesty.

itual reserves in which the manner of choosing a means of transformation is critical. Restricting the act of engenderment to its possible physical meaning, as Ernest Jones does, is to misunderstand the many levels of meaning on which unconscious understandings of procreation engender meaning in the imagination. The coming together of the good objects is multiple in the ways that it can be described. There has to be an interaction between levels of understanding, as in the *Darśan* invocations. 'Becoming', in being inherent in acts of contemplation, depends on there being an oscillation between levels of meaning.

Ritual, as with the making of the circle of light, is related to an unknowable component that is grounded in the realisation that an unknowable (in one form, a spiritual unknowable) is able to absorb into itself the apparently knowable, as in any knowable element in the ritual, including the structures of ritual in themselves. There is an element of that which cannot be explained in transformation, as in the transformation brought about by an act of *Darśan*. Questionably, the divine is similar to an astronomer's black hole in drawing into itself all evidence of creation and all attempts to symbolise the created. The circling light of the Brahmin priest carries within it the meaning of a circling that draws everything into it.

The surface glittered out of a heart of light.

[T. S. ELIOT, *BURNT NORTON*]

There is only one thing that is not an icon of something, and that is nothingness as an absolute metaphysical emptiness.

[EVDOKIMOV, 1972: 237]

A light passes through a stained-glass window. In this case, sunrise and sunset mark the beginning and end of vision. Time enters into an experience whose underlying significance is timeless, as it must in any act of procreation by means of increate light. In the case of the stained-glass window, the meaning of the light that passes through it is of being a natural light; but in its significance it belongs to an aesthetic that is religious, like the imaginary light that lies behind the icon and that pours through its surface and so defines representation as being a form of inward radiance whose source is inaccessible to the one who contemplates it. (There is a strong sense in any attempt to define art to acknowledge a relation between art and prohibition.) The light is inaccessible as other than an inward radiance that the artist can hope to summon up without being able to exercise control over it. The practice of perspective is otherwise. The light no longer shines through the window; it is the perceptor who is the source of light. With the practice of perspective, the perceptor hopes to control the world by means of convergent lines that move towards a dark point into which vision is lost: there is a triumph of the individual over a mystery. With the icon there is no such act of sur-mounting; the attention of the spectator is drawn to a point of light that transforms everything by its radiance. In this way the spectator may hope to enable the mystery to reveal itself by not attempting to control the otherness of its light. The icon is beauty speaking to itself about the nature of a new life to be cherished. The icon is a fact as much about the nature of mind as about the passions that might transform thought and feeling.

In my view, the light that travels through the stained-glass window creates a space inside the cathedral that is similar to a pre-condition for pre-birth states of mind, being within a luminous mind of god from which the Wordsworthian is born with reluctance. Within this earlier place, I imagine there to be prototypes for the two models of perception. An artist may use lines in a perspectival formation to give an image context as well as to give it a semblance of existing within space in its form as a distance. The image does not float: it is retained. It belongs to a system of thought in which objects do not spontaneously appear or disappear. It does not belong to a context of the miraculous, as in the case of the miracle associated with the Holy Sepulchre in Jerusalem, which contains nothing, leaving only a sense of grievous absence. The one who practises perspective – and who in acknowledging the significance of perspective is supported by a culture of immense power – thinks that to hold the image in a certain context is evidence of a mastery: and to some extent it is. Flanked or escorted by lines that move to the same seemingly distant dark point, the image is contained in its journey while being diminished. With the icon, the distant dark point of the perspectival – into which seemingly the image disappears and, in so far as it can be known, is obliterated – reveals its meaning as a point of light that becomes an indefinable effulgence as it would seem to move forward towards the spectator, bathing with light the figures within it.

Nothing in the passing world is invulnerable. Vladimir Lossky, on the roads of France in 1940, meditated on the radiant beauty of cathedrals and other sacred places in a landscape of death and devastation. The artist who practises perspective does not have to think about any conflict between good and evil; it is in the nature of this means of working that it would appear to be above any such conflict. There is no stated antagonism between supporters of thinking by way of perspective and those who dissent from its practice. There is a perennial antagonism in icon thinking between the iconodule and the iconoclast; and it is an error to think that the iconoclast is someone other than myself, either as someone who hates means of representation for one reason or another or as someone who likes to destroy intimations of the beautiful. I assume that there is an iconoclast as well as an iconodule in each of us. The icon carries within a means of visualising the inseparability of good and evil.[5] I have no proof in making this assertion.

Within the cathedral, the stained-glass window is opaque until light begins to pass through it, when it begins to radiate. It is only when I think of the relation of the iconoclast to the stained-glass window that I begin to see the iconic significance that lies within the symbol. The destructive element attacks the meaning of becoming, as when the death of someone capable of being inspired and of inspiring others represents becoming, as in Shelley's reflection on the disabling illness and death of John Keats.

> Life like a dome of many-coloured glass
> Stains the white radiance of Eternity,
> Until Death tramples it to fragments.
>
> [SHELLEY, *ADONAIS: AN ELEGY ON THE DEATH OF JOHN KEATS*]

The breaking of the dome reduces the light of eternity to a white glare that disables the perceptor. 'Stains' could refer to a virtuous means of transmission, or it might refer to the sullied or soiled. The imagery conveys a sense of enduring shock. Milton turned to increase light in the hope that it might compensate for the loss of actual sight. In the world Shelley describes, there is no God and no giving of anonymous donations. To personify the idea of becoming as a form of contemplation, as Keats did, requires that genius

---

[5] For a different kind of meditation on a similar theme, see Natalie Carnes, *Image and Presence* (2018).

should be otherwise endowed. Meister Eckhart refers to an alternative form of becoming, in which acts (like death and the shattering of the dome) are inseparable from an inscrutable kind of giving.

> 'Paul rose from the ground and with open eyes saw nothing' (Acts 9:8). Our masters (Albertus Magnus) say that heaven has a light within itself that does not shine. [...] Seeing nothing, he saw God. The light that is God flows out and darkens every light. [...] In seeing nothing, he saw the divine Nothing.
>
> [IN WALSHE, 2009: 137–141]

Intermediaries enable increate light to represent itself in the world. The dome, whether broken or not, is an intermediary of this kind; it is not the Paraclete. My perception of the heavens by way of it when it was unbroken enables me to perceive the heavens as meaningful because measurable. The poet requires the dome as a means of translating thought from the incomprehensible into the comprehensible if the heavens are in their own way to speak.

> It takes a long performance
> and account to complete the lighting of all the sky-earth:
> The fourfold siding,
> fourfold cornering,
> measuring,
> fourfold staking,
> halving the cord, stretching the cord in the sky,
> on the earth,
> the four sides,
> the four corners, as it is said, by the Maker, Modeler,

Mother,
Father of life,
of humankind,
giver of breath,
giver of heart,
bearer, up-bringer in the light that lasts
of these born in the light, begotten in the light;
worrier, knower of everything, whatever there is:
sky-earth, lake-sea.

[*POPUL VUH* (TEDLOCK, 1985: 6)]

Fascinated by the idea of light, certain leading Flemish painters of the late fourteenth and early fifteenth centuries adopted a strikingly symbolic image that was current in mediaeval thought: theologians and poets often explained the mystery of incarnation by comparing the miraculous conception and birth of Christ to the passage of sunlight through a glass window (Meiss, 1945).

> *St Bernard*: Just as the brilliance of the sun fills and penetrates a glass window without damaging it, and pierces its solid form with imperceptible subtlety, neither hurting it when entering nor destroying it when emerging; thus the word of God, the splendour of the Father, entered the virgin chamber and then came forth from the closed womb.
>
> As the sunbeam through the glass
> Passeth but not staineth
> Thus the Virgin, as she was,
> Virgin still remaineth.

[IN MEISS, 1945]

In one of van Eyck's paintings, daylight fills the church in the same way as increate light filled Mary's womb. A text favoured by Jan van Eyck reads: 'For she is more beautiful than the sun, and above all the orders of the stars; being compared with the light, she is found before it. For she is the brightness of eternal light, and the unspotted mirror of God's majesty.' Van Eyck admired also the text: 'she is the temple of the builder, the sanctuary of the Holy Spirit'.

He must, at the right time, be away – He through whom the
spirit has spoken.

[HÖLDERLIN, *EMPEDOCLES* (IN BULTMANN, 1971)]

Could you but feel his passing needfulness!
Though he himself may dread the hour of drawing nigher,
Already when his words pass earthliness,
He passes with them far beyond your gaze.

[RAINER MARIA RILKE, *SONNETS TO ORPHEUS* 1.5]

The historical Jesus must depart, so that his significance,
the significance of being the one who reveals, can be
grasped purely by itself. He is only the one who reveals,
if he remains such. But he remains such only by send-
ing the [Holy] Spirit, and he can only send the [Holy]
Spirit when he has himself gone. [...] The revelation is
always indirect, but because it occurs within the sphere of
human history it gives rise to the misunderstanding that
it is direct. In order to destroy this misunderstanding,
the one who reveals must take his leave, he must leave
his own in temptation, so that the disciple is freed from
the things that are directly given (which are always slipping away into the past) and turned towards that which
is only indirectly attainable and always in the future. [...]
What was misleading for the first disciples was the illusion of a false certainty which thought that it possessed
the revelation in what was directly given [...] and which

was bound to hope that it would never have an end. The fact that everything is transient was brought home to the disciples by the circumstance that the giver himself goes away. [...] He can only be the one who reveals as the one who is always breaking the given into pieces, always destroying every certainty, always breaking in from the beyond and calling into the future. [...] The Paraclete who is to take his place is always the Word.

[BULTMANN, 1971: 558–560]

This immediate contemporaneity is merely an occasion, which can scarcely be expressed more emphatically than in the proposition that the disciple, if he understood himself, must wish that the immediate contemporaneity so far from being an advantage is one that the contemporary must precisely desire its cessation, lest he be tempted to devote himself to the dangerous toil of seeing and hearing with his bodily eyes and ears.

[KIERKEGAARD, *PHILOSOPHICAL FRAGMENTS* (QUOTED BY BULTMANN, 1971)]

The question is whether an image is not the same as its referent and so expresses the absence of that referent even as it refers to it, or whether it is a site for the *real presence* embodied in the image.

[ELSNER, 2012]

An iconoclast might destroy an icon of Christ on the grounds that Christ was not present in the image, and so think of the image as a form of dissimulation. Or the iconoclast might destroy an icon of Christ on the grounds that Christ *was* present in the image: an idea that disturbingly touches on response at its most primitive.

94

In terms of Rudolph Bultmann's proposal, the argument might be that the image requires a presence of the divine in it if it is to be meaningful. But the divine as inspiration has been and gone, initially leaving grief and an unusual sense of absence as a meaningful communication. In relation to this departure, Rudolph Bultmann perceives the Holy Spirit. A mother in mourning perceives tongues of fire that bear witness to the transforming powers of the Paraclete. Increate light presents itself in unpredictable forms.

*The common function of logos in every system [is] the
reconciliation of the transcendent and immanent views of God.
[...] Logos is the divine fire, the seed from which all birth arises
and into which disintegration brings all things back.*

[R. E. WITT, 1931]

*Grasping anything trustworthy in relation to the soul is
completely and in every way among the most difficult of affairs.*

[ARISTOTLE, *DE ANIMA* 1.402A10–11]

The ritual known as the sacrifice is often assumed to be
intrinsic to cultures that are distant and improbable. The
meaning of the ritual is not discovered in a submerged
way in the present moment. But in Rudolph Bultmann's
perception of a redeemer whose presence and passing has
been unobserved there is an unusual and disturbing depth
related to the meaning of the sacrificial which is no longer
submerged. I am allowed to recognise that a certain experience, no longer accessible, has taken place and in its
immediate potency is incomprehensible. In attempting to
write this book, I thought I was writing about something
(an experience of increate light that others may have had),
and now this something (which does not turn out to be
an experience of increate light) has taken over the writing

and left me partially disabled. A crisis that I thought I was writing about as having taken place elsewhere has become a crisis that has overwhelmed the present.

In terms of Christian thought as I understand it, the sacrifice involves at least three acts: the Crucifixion, which is appalling (and may inform the threatening aspect to Christianity as in the threat of eternal punishment), the harrowing of hell, succeeded by acts of resurrection and final judgment.[1] I came to understand that the idea of an absence that is more potent than any presence is inherent in the succession of narratives, beginning with the Annunciation and followed by the narrative of the Ascension (both being informed by the presence of increate light) and then, almost in negation of these two narratives, two other narratives that are foundational to Christian belief: one being the narrative of the Eucharist, the other being a narrative of an absence more powerful than any presence that is intrinsic to the meaning of the empty sepulchre. The virgin womb, in its association with the potency and literalism of grace, and as foundational (by way of the tongues of fire) to the formation of architectural presence in Christianity, is fundamental to the meaning of a chalice radiant with increate light of the Eucharist and fundamental to the meaning of an empty sepulchre that is radiant with a darkness that is vibrant. The virgin's womb, miraculous in its own way and so unlike the miracle of other wombs, exists in

---

[1] Presumably the people who carried out the Crucifixion did not think they were taking part in a sacrificial rite.

a correlation with an idea of a mouth that knows not what it feeds on – the literal meaning of the transformation within the Eucharist of bread and wine into flesh and blood, a transformation that is analogous to the transforming insemination by light of the Annunciation – and in correlation with the idea of an eye that knows not what it sees – a type of seeing informed by spiritual blindness. To think of these foundational ideas as symbolic of a something other that is possibly evanescent is to misunderstand them. The mouth that knows not on what it feeds and eye that knows not what it sees are literal representations and fundamental to the human condition. Grace, which in its utterance is literalism at its most absolute, is fundamental to the meaning of increate light; and in human terms, grace is a language of the maternal.

At the Last Supper, and by way of the chalice, Christ performs a rite of renewal that in some fundamental way informs all acts of birth: he has bread and wine transform into his own flesh and blood. The mystery of the womb (and indeed of every womb) is synonymous with a mystery of the mouth in which the presence of god lies on the feeder's tongue. Meanwhile, the authority of the empty sepulchre centres on the womb-like idea of the dead being reborn in a context in which absence is more potent than any presence.

The philosopher G.F.W. Hegel came close to comparing literal and symbolic interpretations of the Eucharist with literal and symbolic understandings among the first followers of Zoroaster (which brings this book back full circle to its beginning). I think that Hegel, who is mysterious in his way of writing, argues in favour for the symbolic as against the literal.

> The inventor of shapes must unfold their inner core adequately [*namely, by means of symbolism*], Religion has its source in the spirit, which seeks its own truth, has some inkling of it, and brings the same before our minds in some shape or other more closely or more distantly related to this truthful content.
>
> [HEGEL, *AESTHETICS*, 1975: 310–311]

> In Catholic doctrine, for example, the consecrated bread is the actual flesh, the wine the actual blood of God, and Christ is immediately present in them; and even in the Lutheran faith bread and wine are transformed by the believer's enjoyment [*enjoyment, really?*] into actual flesh and blood. In this mystical identity there is nothing purely symbolical; the latter only arises in the Reformed (namely, Calvinist) doctrine, because there the spiritual is explicitly severed from the sensuous, and the external object is taken in that case as a mere pointing to a meaning differentiated therefrom. [...]
>
> [*IBID.*: 324]

> We find this wholly immediate unity in the life and religion of the ancient Zend people whose ideas and institutions are preserved for us in the Zen Avesta. The religion of Zoroaster takes light as it exists in nature – the sun, the stars, fire in its luminosity and flames – to be the Absolute, without explicitly separating the Divinity from Light, as if light were a mere expression and image or

symbol. The Divine, the meaning, is not separated from its existence, from the lights. [...] (Light) is not thought at all to be a mere image of the good; on the contrary, the good itself is light.

[*IBID.*: 325 ET SEQ.]

A cosmos without music is unimaginable: arguably even if I were deaf, I would like to think that my mind might encompass the idea of music as a presence. In the same way that I think to recognise a light of the mind that has no source in nature, I might still think to recognise an aural analogue to the visual light of the mind. (This is the light that St Augustine identifies with God.) But let me suppose that there is an absence of music as a form of knowledge or as a type of experience. I would not recognise the absence, because there would be no clue as to what the idea of music might realise if it were to assume being. I would live in absence and be insensible to the meaning of the absence.

Let me now imagine that music as a culture and realisation is suddenly made apparent as a totality; it surrounds me and embraces me; it has always been there, and I have been unable to see it. I am ascribing a spiritual conversion to an object rather than the subject of a conversion; it is not 'me' that changes; it is 'it' that changes.[2] At this point, music as a culture and as a realisation reveals itself to be inherent in the cosmos (which is my present belief, which I assume with

---

[2] The god whose sight formerly blinded me is now the god who is blinded in recognising me. The meaning of the blinding has been transferred.

complacence. I am not critically aware of the fact that music is a gift that is either given to me or taken away from me).

The absence and presence of music are examples of the operations of grace rather than examples of the operations of nature: that is, my understanding of music as a natural fact like other objects in nature is based on a misunderstanding that leads me to be insensitive to the actions of grace as a motive. The deep nature of the meaning concerning whether or not music is part of the cosmos supposes that I am able to see the tongues of fire, which in fact I am unable to do; I am unable to see the workings of grace.

The act of transubstantiation is like the culture and realisation of a music that I had no idea existed. The concept of transformation, which I had thought to be a concept that operated within the terms of nature and so shows itself to be fallacious, shows itself to be a concept that operates within the terms of grace. By means of grace, intimacy is secured, and bread and wine actually transform into the flesh and blood of a sacred being. To have this truth weigh down on one is an unwelcome experience. A subsidiary feature of this transformation is to reveal that, apart from symbolic and literal interpretations of meaning, there is a semantic of the sacrifice, in which the improbable reforms itself as the real.

In thy light we shall see light.

[PSALM 35.10]

Who covers thyself with light as with a garment [...] who walks upon the wings of the wind.

[PSALM 104]

Attempting to write about the absence that is greater than the presence itself, which Rudolph Bultmann has described as the continuing presence of the departed Redeemer, I was inclined to think of this idea as being an emptiness where a fullness in meaning might have been. I was unable at the time to see how a semantic based on an idea of the sacrifice might be neither a symbolic nor a literal idea.

> They departed, although they were dwelling in the core of my heart.
>
> [IBN ARABĪ (IN JAMAL, 2010: 104)]

The centre is lost. 'Jerusalem Athens Alexandria Vienna London' (to misquote T.S. Eliot, 1922) have become 'unreal'. What had once been an out-pouring of meaning is now an obscured source of communication. In place of the symbol, there is the relic, a form of the fetish, a rind without fruit. Mourning supposes a psychic centre in time and space in relation to which there has been a loss. As against this sense, think of a text whose meaning requires the unusual condition that the author is always present or the text disappears. The document is no longer an object in history; it no longer has the underlying continuity of an informing ground. But, as Rudolf Bultmann indicates, those who are abandoned are not totally so; grace, the Mother of the Burning Bush, beauty itself, is present, although at times in imperceptible ways. The source of contemplation re-forms into a symbol that arises from a hinterland to meaning: the Annunciation narrative, which is as much a narrative about love at first sight as it is about a unique engenderment, leads through the narrative of the Assumption to a world in which a chalice–womb radiant with increate light presents itself as a means of redemption. But then the chalice disappears, or, rather, the idea of a lost grail becomes its phantom representation. And the way to and from the empty sepulchre has become uncertain.

> Sometime in the late twelfth century, Chrétien de Troyes wrote the story of the Grail. This unfinished work, with its castle and ailing king, bleeding lance, and platter of gold, impressed itself on those who came to know it, fostering a host of authors who reworked its story. Writing ten years or so after Chrétien, Robert de Boron first connected the Grail to the vessel of the Last Supper, which he claimed was given to Joseph of Arimathea by Pilate to collect the blood of the crucified Christ. According to the Vulgate *Estoire*, Joseph brought it to England, where

(as reported by the monks) he founded the first Christian church and was buried in the confines of the abbey, near to what would become celebrated as King Arthur's tomb. The religious Grail mixed the historical and secular one, complicated the message between successive retellings. As the legend grew and its theology developed, the two Grails overlapped in ways that would prove forever problematic.

[BRASWELL, 2011: 470]

Joseph of Arimathea, possibly an uncle of Christ, but possibly no more than a fiction, personifies the idea of transmission. He carries the idea of a lengthy traversal from centre to periphery as associated with a loss and misunderstanding. He bears witness to the Last Supper and the first enactment by Christ of the transubstantiation theme. The claim is that with the same chalice, he collects blood from the wound that Longinus inflicted on Christ. He is the owner of the tomb in which the dead Christ was laid and from which he disappeared as the earliest stage in a resurrection. He is thought to have attended the Last Supper and to have seen in an act of transubstantiation an enactment of the meaning of the sacrifice. The notion of sanctity as having a centre and periphery is disabled (the repeated failure of the Crusades diminished any claim to identify Jerusalem with Christian idealism). The sense of an Alice in Wonderland logic takes over.[1] The chalice disappears; its place in reverie is taken by

---

[1] 'Often when two buildings are compared with one another in medieval writings the modern reader may wonder how the author came to see any resemblance between

the grail, which shines with a supernatural light. The grail, whether vessel or platter, disappears. (As platter it intimates the meaning of the vessel on which lay in pools of blood the decapitated head of John the Baptist.)

The problem that faces Parsifal, the hero of the Chrétien de Troyes' story, concerns a question that no one asks and an answer that no one is able to give. For William Blake, the waste land of the grail romances was a land that the 'dark satanic mills' of industrialisation had laid waste to, rather than a land destroyed by a natural blight. In one account, Blake went to Glastonbury in an attempt to find the lost grail. The centre associated with the one-time potent radiance of the revelatory was still Jerusalem, but, as Rudolf Bultmann's intuition would indicate, the source of revelation was no more than a potent absence. However, grace in all its elusive sufficiency remained.[2]

---

the two. The tenth-century *Miracula S. Maximini*, for instance, records that the church at Germigny-des-Prés was built like the palatine chapel at Aix-la-Chapelle. [...] Since two of these edifices still exist [...] it is easy to check these examples; yet it is hard for a modern beholder to see anything comparable to them. [...] One might at first be inclined to say that these statements are based simply on mistakes; but they are made so frequently and with such precision that this explanation seems too easy an escape' (Krautheimer, 1942: 2).

[2] In this model, the mother is helpless in the face of a struggle for redemption.

The act of procreation – so potent in meaning – appears to engage with different levels of understanding. The formula of *logos plus semina aeternitatis* (a Stoic concept signifying the seed of eternity) *plus increate light* describes, in a kind of shorthand, the act of sexual generation as an approximate to the sacred. The way in which it related to biological acts of procreation is obscure.

Thinking of this kind occurs on a paternal level. I began to write this book with a formula of this sort in mind. I bring it to an end with an alternation in gender and with a maternal interpretation of the formula as beauty plus increate light plus grace. The presence of grace in this definition is unnerving as well as astonishing; it is a pointer to why the presence of beauty in being inseparable from a presence of increate light can be so disturbing. Grace eludes understanding. Like many interpretations of the divine, it is not a concept in epistemology; and yet it is as present in the world I live in as the air I breathe. It informs wonder. I sense that it joins and unjoins spiritual links in the mind in ways that cannot be explained.

It belongs to a type of nucleus in thought that would seek to invite interpretation and yet that continues to be elusive, tantalising and unapproachable. Essentially, it presents itself as a yearning to realise itself the world in a way that resists definition, as a reaching out that at the same time is a means of retreat. I am inclined to believe that it is a form of the face that no one can look on and live (Exodus 33:20).

It points to one of the cruxes of religious intuition that are analogues to the source of procreated life in the virgin womb in being forms of absence as presence or forms of presence as absence. It is like a language that I feel I have long known and yet that continues to remains foreign to me. The argument is inviting that it has a likeness to something that cannot be understood, like the meaning of transubstantiation in the Eucharist or like the meaning of trauma in psychoanalysis. A meaning resists explication while continuing to emit a sense of being significant (Marcus Pound, 2007). Something yearns to be deciphered that in its yearning obstructs any evolution into meaning: there is an effective resistance to any attempt to release a sense of evidence into a possible experience.[1]

Rudolph Bultmann perceives a presence in absence in the painful realisation that revelation belongs to a time that has passed and not to a time that is present; the relation of revelation to the world is one of something being essential to the world that has departed from it, so that any hint of

---

[1] Hegel was unsure as to whether the rites of transubstantiation, which he described in relation to the thought of the earliest Zoroastrians, should be thought of as forms of symbolism or as forms of literalism (He was convinced that the Zoroastrians in their literalism made no distinction between the presence of increate light and the good: the two were inseparable aspects of each other; he gave no opinion on the meaning of the Eucharist.) I am suggesting that there is a third way of interpreting that which insists on being interpreted and that resists any attempt at interpretation.

the revelatory is inseparable from intimations of grief.[2] The assumption is that all enactments of this kind have the form of reminiscence. I incline to disagree.

I infer from this mode of perception a certain way of interpreting the meaning of the two ongoing miracles that revelation in its departure has endowed the remaining world – one being the mystery of the Eucharist, the other the mystery of the empty sepulchre – as symbolic rather than as literal. It obliges me to think about time as a fateful impress like a passing over of the angel of death (a thought that is inherent in Rudolph Bultmann's vision). I find the perception both convincing and unconvincing. The relation of the two mysteries to time is no more than partial. Can there be a departure in relation to them or do they continue to have being outside the context of temporal measure? As Hooker says in his *Laws* (2.247). 'We take not baptism nor the Eucharist for bare resemblances or memorials of things absent' (in Holtzen, 2011: 628). Or, as Martin Luther said concerning the transformation of natural substances into spiritual ones, 'We take not the waters of baptism to be like the water that a maid-servant throws over a cow.' Transformations that cannot be related to time have a built-in intensity in meaning that would have them be understood in a way that resists understanding. This is one of the meanings concerning the

---

[2] If I believe in the transubstantiation of the Eucharist literally rather than metaphorically, then I am unlikely to think of revelation as a passing event.

realisation that the coming together of beauty and increate light is meaningful because it is informed by grace.

And it is also the meaning of a particular virgin's womb. Tongues of fire that cross a night-time sky intimate its presence. A mother in mourning bears witness to a different kind of creation, one that signals in the wilderness the possible formation of new cultures and insights on a land that is otherwise waiting for a spiritual insemination. On a much later occasion, enemy planes spat tongues of fire over a landscape and devastated it and destroyed many people: evidence that Vladimir Lossky had reason to grieve over as he made his way across France in June, 1940.

So with the lamps put out, the moon sunk, and a thin
rain drumming on the roof, a downpouring of immense
darkness began. […] A random light from an uncovered
star, or wandering ship, or the Lighthouse even, directed
pale footfalls upon stair and mat. The little airs mounted the
staircase and nosed around bedroom doors. And here surely
they must cease. Whatever else may perish and disappear,
what lies here is steadfast. Here one might say to those lights
that slide, those fumbling airs that breathe and bend over the
bed itself, here you can neither touch nor destroy.

[VIRGINIA WOOLF. *TO THE LIGHTHOUSE*. 1927: 115-116
(WITH A SLIGHT ADJUSTMENT TO THE TEXT)]

beauty: grace: increate light

References

Aaron, D. H. (1997). Shedding light on God's body in Rabbinic Midrashim. *Harvard Theological Review, 90* (3): 299–314.

Allen, M. J. B. (Ed.) (2015). *Marsilio Ficino. On Dionysius the Areopagite, Volume 1: Mystical Theology.* Cambridge, MA: Harvard University Press.

Armstrong, A. H. (1937). 'Emanation' in Plotinus. *Mind, 46* (181): 61–66.

Asher, C. B. (2004). A ray from the sun. In M. Kapstein (Ed.), *The Presence of Light: Divine Radiance and Religious Experience.* Chicago, IL: University of Chicago Press.

Assmann, J. (1995). *Egyptian Solar Religion in the New Kingdom: Re, Amun and the Crisis of Polytheism.* London: Kegan Paul.

Bady, G. (2013). La lumière, image de Dieu et nom de l'homme chez Grégoire de Nazianze. *Revue des Sciences Philosophiques et Théologiques, 97* (4): 459–476.

Boyce, M. (1964). *Textual Sources for the Study of Zoroastrianism.* Manchester: Manchester University Press.

Boyce, M. (1979). *Zoroastrians: Their Religious Beliefs and Practices.* London: Routledge, 2001.

Braswell, M. A. (2011). The search for the Holy Grail: Arthurian Lacunae in the England of Edward III. *Studies in Philology, 108* (4): 469–487.

Brouyer, L. (1960). *Introduction to the Spiritual Life.* Notre Dame, IN: Ave Maria Press, 2013.

Brown, S. F. (Ed.) (1993). *Bonaventure of Bagnoregio: Journey of the Mind to God*, trans P. Boehner. Indianapolis, IN: Hackett.

Bucur, B. G. (2008). Foreordained from all eternity: The mystery of the incarnation according to some early Christian and Byzantine writers. *Dumbarton Oaks Papers, 62*: 199–215.

Bulgakov, S. (1926). *The Burning Bush: On the Orthodox Veneration of the Mother of God*, trans. T. A. Smith. Grand Rapids, MI: Eerdmans, 2009.

Bultmann, R. (1971). *The Gospel of John: A Commentary.* Eugene, OR: Wipf & Stock.

Carnes, N. (2018). *Image and Presence: A Christological Reflection on Iconoclasm and Iconophilia.* Stanford, CA: Stanford University Press.

Casas, G. (2014). Les statues vivent aussi. Theorie néoplatonicinne de l'objet rituel. *Revue de L'histoire des Religions, 231*: 663–679.

Clark, M. (2019). *Soma* and *Hoama*: Ayahuasca analogues from the Later Bronze Age. *Journal of Psychedelic Studies, 3* (2): 104–116.

Clément, O. (1964). *Byzance et le christianisme.* Paris: Desclée de Brouwer.

Corbin, H. (1958). *Creative Imagination in the Sūfism of Ibn 'Arabī*, trans. R. Manheim. London: Routledge & Kegan Paul, 1970.

Corbin, H. (1960). *Spiritual Body and Celestial Earth. From Mazdean Iran to Shī'ite Iran.* Princeton, NJ: Bollingen, 1977.

Corbin, H. (1994). *The Man of Light in Iranian Sufism.* New Lebanon, NY: Omega.

Cottingham, J., Stoothoff, R., & Murdoch, D. (1984). *The Philosophical Writings of Descartes, Vol. 2.* Cambridge: Cambridge University Press.

Cottingham, J., Stoothoff, R., & Murdoch, D. (1985). *The Philosophical Writings of Descartes, Vol. 1.* Cambridge: Cambridge University Press.

Daniélou, J. (1962). *From Glory to Glory*, trans. H. Musurillo. London: John Murray.

de Chardin, P. T. (1968). *The Divine Milieu: An Essay on the Interior Life.* New York: Harper & Row.

Dupey García, E. (2015). The materiality of color in the body ornamentation of the Aztec gods. *RES: Anthropology and Aesthetics, 65/66*: 72–88.

Eck, D. L. (1998). *Darśan: Seeing the Divine Image in India.* New York: Columbia University Press.

Eliot, T. S. (1922). *The Waste Land*. New York: Boni & Liveright,

Elsner, J. (2012). Iconoclasm as discourse: From Antiquity to Byzantium. *The Art Bulletin, 94* (3): 368–394.

Evdokimov, P. (1972). *The Art of the Icon: A Theology of Beauty*. Torrance, CA: Oakwood, 1990.

Florensky, P. (1996). *Iconostasis*. Crestwood, NY: St Vladimir's Seminary Press.

Golding, W. (1979). *Darkness Visible*. London: Faber & Faber.

Gregory of Nyssa (1978). *The Life of Moses*. New York: Paulist Press.

Hegel, G. F. W. (1975). *Aesthetics: Lectures on Fine Art, Volume 1*, trans. T. M. Knox. Oxford: Clarendon Press, 2014.

Heinrich, C. (1995). *Strange Fruit: Alchemy, Religion and Magical Foods. A Speculative History*. London: Bloomsbury.

Hilton, W. (1957). *The Ladder of Perfection*. London: Penguin, 1988.

Holtzen, T. L. (2011). Sacramental causality in Hooker's Eucharistic theology. *Journal of Theological Studies, 62* (2): 607–648.

Jamal, M. (Ed.). (2010). *Islamic Mystical Poetry*. London: Penguin Classics.

James, M. R. (2004). *The New Testament Apocrypha*. Berkeley, CA: Apochryphile Press.

Kozin, A. V. (2007). Iconic wonder: Pavel Florensky's phenomenology of the face. *Studies in East European Thought, 59* (4): 293–308.

Kramrisch, S. (1981). *The Presence of Shiva*. Princeton, NJ: Princeton University Press.

Krautheimer, R. (1942). Introduction to an 'Iconography of Mediaeval Architecture'. *Journal of the Warburg and Courtauld Institutes, 5*.

Lau, D. C. (Trans. & Ed.) (1963). *Lao Tzu: Tao Te Ching*. London: Penguin, 1985.

Lossky, V. (1944). *The Mystical Theology of the Eastern Church*. Crestwood, NY: St Vladimir's Seminary Press, 1957.

Lossky, V. (1959). *In the Image and Likeness of God*. Crestwood, NY: St Vladimir's Seminary Press, 1974.

Lossky, V. (Trans.) (1998). *Sept jours sur les routes de France: Juin 1940*. Paris: Editions du Cerf.

Luibheid, C. (Trans.) (1987). *Pseudo-Dionysius: The Complete Works.* Mahwah, NJ: Paulist Press.

Malebranche, N. (1674). *Search after Truth.* Cambridge: Cambridge University Press, 2006.

Meiss, M. (1945). Light as form and symbol in some fifteenth-century paintings. *The Art Bulletin, 27* (3): 176–181.

Melamed, Y. Y. (2016). *Eternity: A History.* New York: Oxford University Press.

Meyendorff, J. (1959). *A Study of Gregory Palamas.* Crestwood, NY: St Vladimir's Seminary Press, 1998.

Meyendorff, J. (Ed.) (1974). *St Gregory Palamas and Orthodox Spirituality.* Crestwood, NY: St Vladimir's Seminary Press.

Meyendorff, J. (Ed.). (1983). *St Gregory Palamas: The Triads.* Mahwah, NJ: Paulist Press.

Minnis, A. J. (1983). Affection and imagination in *The Cloud of Unknowing* and Hilton's *Scale of Perfection. Traditio, 39*: 323–366.

Morley, R. (1975). Negative theology and abstraction in Plotinus. *American Journal of Philology, 96* (4): 363–377.

Muller-Ortega, P. E. (2004). Luminous consciousness: Light in the tantric mysticism of Abhinavagupta. In M. Kapstein (Ed.), *The Presence of Light: Divine Radiance and Religious Experience.* Chicago, IL: University of Chicago Press.

Nes, S. (2007). *The Uncreated Light. An Iconographical Study of the Transfiguration in the Eastern Church.* Grand Rapids, MI: Eerdmans.

Newman, B. (2005). What did it mean to say 'I saw'? The clash between theory and practice in Medieval visionary culture. *Speculum, 80* (1): 1–43.

Onians, R. B. (1951). *The Origins of European Thought about the Body, the Mind, the Soul, the Word, Time & Fate.* Cambridge: Cambridge University Press.

Orlov, A., & Golitzin, A. (2001). 'Many Lamps Are Lightened from the One': Paradigms of the transformational vision of Macarian homilies. *Vigiliae Christianae, 55* (3): 281–298.

Pound, M. (2007). Eucharist and trauma. *New Blackfriars, 88* (1014): 187–194.

Propp, H. C. (Trans. & Ed.) (1999). *Exodus 1–18.* New Haven, CT: Yale University Press, 2010.

Radhakrishnan, S., & Moore, C. A. (1957). *A Source Book in Indian Philosophy.* Princeton, NJ: Princeton University Press, 1973.

Renou, L. (1952). On the Word Âtmàn. *Vak* 2: 151–157. [Reprinted in N. Balbir & G.-J. Pinault, *Louis Renou. Choix d'études indiennes.* Paris: École Française, 1997.]

Ries, J. (1991). Dieux cosmiques et Dieu Biblique dans la religion de Mani. *Augustiana, 4*: 757–772.

Rodziewicz, A. (2016). And the pearl became an egg: The Yezidi Red Wednesday and its cosmogonic background. *Iran and the Caucasus* [Special Issue: Studies on Ethno-Religious Groups], 20 (3/4): 347–367.

Scholem, G. (1956). The meaning of the Torah in Jewish mysticism. *Diogenes, 4*: 36–47.

Tedlock, D. (Trans.) (1985). *Popul Vuh: The Mayan Book of the Dawn of Life.* New York: Touchstone, 1996.

Traherne, T. (1906). 'The Third Century.' In *Centuries of Meditations.* Grand Rapids, MI: Christian Classics Ethereal Library. London: Bertram Lobell.

Trouillard, J. (1972). Rencontre de Néoplatonisme. *Revue de Théologie et Philosophie, 3rd Series, 22* (1).

Walbridge, J., & Ziai, H. (Trans. & Ed.) (1999). *Suhrawardi: The Philosophy of Illumination.* Provo, UT: Brigham Young University Press.

Waley, A. (1958). *The Way and Its Power: Lao Tzu's Tao Te Ching and Its Place in Chinese Thought.* New York: Grove Press.

Walshe, M. O'C. (Trans. & Ed.) (2009). *The Complete Mystical Works of Meister Eckhart.* Chestnut Ridge, NY: Crossroad Publishing.

Weil, S. (2019). *Ecrits de New York et de Londres.* Paris: Gallimard.

White, C. H. (2017). *New Collected Poems of Marianne Moore.* New York: Farrar, Straus & Giroux.

Wineman, A. (2019). Metamorphoses of the hidden light motifs in Jewish texts. *Hebrew Studies, 60*: 323–332.

Witt, R. E. (1931). The Plotinian Logos and its Stoic basis. *The Classical Quarterly, 25* (2): 103–111.

Woolf, V. (1927). *To the Lighthouse.* London: Folio Society, 1988.

Zajonc, A. (1955). *Catching the Light: The Entwined History of Light and Mind.* New York: Oxford University Press, 1993.

Index

For Maria

And with thanks to friends who helped me improve the text